WHITEFIELD
GOLD

WHITEFIELD
GOLD

COMPILED BY RAY COMFORT

Bridge-Logos

Gainesville, Florida 32614

Bridge-Logos

Gainesville, FL 32614 USA

Whitefield Gold

by Ray Comfort

Library of Congress Catalog Card Number: 2005936841
International Standard Book Number 0-88270-079-0

Unless otherwise indicated, Scripture quotations are from the Holy Bible: King James Version.

G163.316.N.m601.35260

My sincere thanks to www.thegreatnews.com
for their assistance with research and to
Judy Notchick for her research.

Table of Contents

Foreword

For many years I have often quoted George Whitefield, and spoken with high regard about his open air preaching. However, it was only after reading (in this compilation) of his deep passion for the lost and his incredible love for God, that I fell in love with him as a brother in Christ.

It is said that he wept as he preached to the lost. I believe that it was because he had an eternal and biblically based perspective. Most modern preachers preach Christ for this life. Whitefield preached Jesus for the next—as Him who saves us from wrath that is to come. He stubbornly preached the truth in love, and multitudes flocked to hear him.

May we sit at his feet and learn.

Ray Comfort

George Whitefield
1714-1769

Itinerant Evangelist
"Trumpet of the Great Awakening"

George Whitefield (pronounced *Whitfield*), son of an innkeeper, was not an imposing figure. Slight of build, cross-eyed, and the youngest of seven children, he received more than his fair share of knocks and torments. But God gives each of us at least one talent, and to George Whitefield, that talent was a voice—a voice like a trumpet, a voice like a lion, a voice that could be heard a mile away, a voice that could shake walls, rattle windows, and create tears to run down the soot-covered cheeks of the coldest, hardest coalminers of the day. Whitefield did not discover this talent until he was nineteen, but once discovered, he never hid it away or neglected the great gift God gave him.

England in the early 1700s was a vile, cruel, inhuman place. Drunkenness had become such an epidemic that imported liquor was banned. This ruling only fueled the "homemade gin craze" that caused more inhumanity, insanity, and cruelty. Public hangings were considered "festivals," and they were frequent due to the fact that 160 different offenses carried the death penalty. Hangings did nothing to lower the crime rate, and the only things that flourished in England were the prisons. The church was the Church of England, but religion was as cold, dreary, and lacking in hope or charity as the infamous slums of London.

Into this forbidding world, George Whitefield was born in 1714 at the Bell Inn and Tavern in Gloucester, England. His father was the innkeeper and the Bell was the grandest establishment in town. It had two halls, one of which was used for stage plays. George's father died when he was only two, but his mother tried to keep the business going with the help of an older son. Even at a young age, George tended bar and was a favorite of the customers. He entertained them with impersonations, including a good impersonation of the local pastor. His mother remarried after six years, but this marriage was a mistake, and the inn was in deep financial trouble. George had started school when he was twelve, but quit when he was fifteen to help run the family business. George was gifted in school (when he wasn't truant), but loved speaking and acting in school assemblies and plays the most.

Searching and Thirsting

Although forced to leave school, George continued reading and learning on his own. He would don his old blue apron and wash dishes, clean rooms, and draw beer by day, and read his Bible and classics by night. By the time he was 16, he could read Latin and some Greek. His mother always wanted her youngest to attend college, but knew it was impossible because there was no money. One day a customer came into the tavern and described to George and his mother how he had attended Oxford University as a "servitor." Servitors were poor students who worked for rich students. George eagerly accepted the challenge, and in 1732 at the age of 17, he entered Pembroke College at Oxford.

The life of a servitor was much like that of an indentured servant. Servitors served three or four higher students and did whatever they wanted done: washing clothes, shining shoes, completing homework, or running errands. George had to wear a special gown, and regular students could not speak to him. He was not permitted to associate with other students or join clubs or take part in activities. Most servitors could not endure the constant humiliation and left college. George persevered by becoming extremely devout in his Bible study and prayers, and by visiting prisoners and poorhouses. He had heard of a large group of religious students called "the Holy Club," but had never met them and was not allowed to approach them. However, one of the founders of the club, Charles Wesley, had heard of George's devotion, and broke tradition by inviting him to join the group.

Members of the Holy Club were mockingly called "Methodists" because of their highly disciplined and structured lifestyle. But the lifestyle practiced by John and Charles Wesley and the other members of the club appealed to George, and he quickly became their most devoted and hardest working member. George discovered a book by Rev. Henry Scougal, "The Life of God in the Soul of Man," that showed him that all of his good deeds, service and fasting were for naught unless he had Christ formed "within" him and was born again.

This book shook George's faith to the core. He wanted to be born again, but did not know how. He fasted more, gave his money away, dressed in rags, and spent all night in prayer. He spoke to no one and withdrew from the Holy Club. His studies faltered until he was threatened with expulsion. It appears that he had an emotional breakdown and suffered from severe depression. Other students thought he was mad and threw dirt at him. For Lent that year he ate only a little bread and tea. He became so sick and emaciated that a physician was called, and George was confined to bed for seven weeks. During this convalescence, George finally surrendered to God and cried out for help. "I thirst," he moaned from his bed. He said it was like a floodgate opening, and he felt profound joy and release. He was reborn!

Still ill in body, George returned home to Gloucester for nine months of recuperation. But he was a new man with a new mission. He knew he no longer needed to win God's favor, but he did need to continually serve God. He started a small society that met nightly for study and prayer. His religious devotion attracted the attention of the Bishop of Gloucester who offered to ordain him as a deacon even though he was not of the required age. George feared that he was not ready for ordination, but vowed that he would be ordained if somehow he received funds to return to Oxford and graduate. Money slowly appeared from relatives and churches along with news from Oxford that the Wesley brothers had left to become missionaries in America, and George Whitefield was needed to become the leader of the Holy Club. Whitefield returned to Oxford, graduated, and was ordained as a deacon in 1736. He was 21.

Creating Madness and Enthusiasm

Whitefield preached his very first sermon in the church in Gloucester were he had been baptized and reared as a child. He preached with such eloquence and authority that someone complained to the Bishop that he had driven fifteen people mad. The Bishop calmly replied that he hoped the madness would not be forgotten before the next Sunday.

Whitefield stayed at Oxford and started studying for his Master's degree, but as soon as he started preaching, requests for his services overwhelmed him. Within four weeks, he had preached at Gloucester, Bath, and Bristol to packed churches. Thousands more mobbed the streets to see and hear him, since none of the churches was large enough for the throngs. He had started a small revival and caused a bigger uproar. As soon as the Church of England heard of his success and the fact that he was calling for all to be reborn (even the clergy!), they began to persecute him and declare that he was guilty of "enthusiasm." Ordained clergy were expected to be sedate, quiet, and apparently boring. Whitefield's eloquent, expressive, extemporaneous style was closer to a performance than a sermon, and the Church of England wanted nothing to do with it.

But just as Whitefield's ministry was increasing exponentially every week, he received a request from John Wesley to travel to the colony of Georgia in America to become a missionary. He accepted the challenge and sailed to Savannah. Sailing across the Atlantic was a perilous trip that took two months in good weather and up to three or four months in usual weather. Even though Whitefield was never in good health, he made a total of seven trips to America, crossing the Atlantic thirteen times, and spending a total of over two years at sea. This never slowed down his preaching as he presented sermons every day aboard ship, along with prayer and Bible study. In Georgia, he founded schools and an orphanage named Bethesda [meaning *House of Mercy*] that still exists today. He returned to England after only four months to find that his ministry was still growing, but his pulpit-space was disappearing.

He was ordained as a priest in the Church of England in Oxford, but when he went to London, only four churches would let him in the door. He preached wherever he was allowed and spoke to societies and prisoners, nobility and shopkeepers. But as his crowds and popularity grew, the Church became more antagonistic.

Whitefield then did the unthinkable for an ordained minister. He preached outdoors! Not only was open air preaching unacceptable, undignified, and dirty, it was illegal. Preaching was to be done only in "consecrated buildings." The only exception was for public hangings, were Whitefield often preached, frequently delaying the execution while the crowds stood, riveted to his every word of repentance and forgiveness.

Despite these prohibitions, in 1739, Whitefield set out for Kingswood, a poor coal-mining area near Bristol. It was a freezing, February day, but he walked through the dirt streets and found 200 people willing to listen to him. He told them about the love of Jesus and how Jesus had died for them. The next day, 2,000 people showed up, and by Sunday more than 10,000 people appeared from all over the area. Whitefield started a young people's meeting in his sister's house with 50 people, and within 6 weeks he had over 5,000 filling the village green. Whitefield preached in the open all over England that spring and summer, and spoke to over two million people. The churches were closed, but the people were open to the Word of God.

Whitefield left this great revival in the hands of John and Charles Wesley to return to America in August 1739. Regional revivals were already appearing in America under the leadership of William Tennant and his sons in Pennsylvania and Jonathon Edwards in New England. Whitefield ignited these revivals into a continent–wide "Great Awakening." He spoke in every city, town, and village green, morning, noon, and night. He preached to over 35,000 in Philadelphia, 20,000 in New York and 20,000 in Boston. The name of George

Whitefield was the most recognized name on the North American continent, not only because of the news of his preaching, but because he had met face-to-face with more people in America than any other single person of that era. Even George Washington was just a young boy contemplating cherry trees when Whitefield stormed through Virginia. When he tried to travel south to Georgia, over 1,000 people followed him, and he had to stop at every village to preach. It took him over two months on horseback and canoe to reach Savannah. A local farmer vividly describes how this fervor spread throughout America:

The Spiritual Travels of Nathan Cole

I was born Feb. 15ᵗʰ 1711 and born again Oct. 1741- When I was young I had very early Convictions, but after I grew up I was an Arminian until I was near 30 years of age; I intended to be saved by my own works such as prayers and good deeds.

Now it pleased God to send Mr. Whitefield into this land; and my hearing of his preaching at Philadelphia, like one of the Old Apostles, and many thousands flocking to hear him preach the Gospel; and great numbers were converted to Christ, I felt the Spirit of God drawing me by conviction. I longed to see and hear him, and wished he would come this way. I heard he was come to New York and the Jerseys and great multitudes flocking after him under great concern for their Souls which brought on my Concern more and more hoping soon to see him but next I heard he was at Long Island, then at Boston and next at Northampton.

Then on a Sudden, in the morning about 8 or 9 of the Clock there came a messenger and said Mr. Whitefield preached at Hartford and Weathersfield yesterday and is to preach at Middletown this morning at ten of the Clock. I was in my field at Work. I dropped my tool that I had in my hand and went home to my wife telling her to make ready to go and hear Mr. Whitefield preach at Middletown, then run to my pasture for my horse. I with my wife soon mounted the horse and went forward as fast as I thought the horse could bear, and when my horse got much out of breath I would get down and put my wife on the Saddle and bid her ride as fast as she could and not Stop or Slack for me except I bade her and so I would run until I was much out of breath, and then mount my horse again, and so I did several times to favor the horse; we improved every moment to get along as if we were fleeing for our lives; all the while fearing we should be too late to hear the Sermon, for we had twelve miles to ride double in little more than an hour and we went up and by the upper housen parish.

And when we came within about half a mile or a mile of the Road that comes down from Hartford Weathersfield and Stepney to Middletown, on high land before me I saw a Cloud of fog rising; I first thought it came from the great River [the Connecticut River], but as I came nearer the Road, I heard a noise something like a low rumbling thunder and presently found it was the noise of Horses feet coming down the Road and this Cloud was a Cloud of dust made by the Horses feet; it arose some Rods into the air over the tops of Hills and trees, and when I came within about 20 rods of the Road, I could see men and horses Slipping along the Cloud like shadows and as I drew nearer it seemed like a steady Stream of horses and their riders, scarcely a horse more than his length behind another, all of a Lather and foam with sweat, their breath rolling out of their nostrils every Jump, every horse seemed to go with all his might to carry his rider to hear news from heaven for the saving of Souls. It made me tremble to see the Sight, how the world was in a Struggle, I found a Vacancy between two horses to Slip in mine and my Wife said how our Clothes will be all spoiled see how they look, for they were so Covered with dust, that they looked almost all of a Color Coats, hats, Shirts, and horses.

We went down in the Stream but heard no man speak a word all the way for 3 miles but every one pressing forward in great haste and when we got to Middletown old meeting house there was a great Multitude it was said to be 3 or 4,000 of people Assembled together; we dismounted and shook off our Dust; and the ministers were then Coming to the meeting house. I turned and looked towards the Great River and saw the ferry boats Running swift backward and forward bringing over loads of people and the Oars Rowed nimble and quick, every thing, men horses and boats seemed to be Struggling for life. The land and banks over the river looked black with people and horses all along the twelve miles I saw no man at work in his field, but all seemed to be gone.

When I saw Mr. Whitefield, come upon the Scaffold he looked almost angelical; a young, slim, slender, youth before some thousands of people with a bold undaunted Countenance, and my hearing how God was with him every where as he came along it solemnized my mind, and **put me into a trembling fear** before he began to preach; for he looked as if he was clothed with authority from the Great God; and a sweet solemnity sat upon his brow. And my hearing him preach, gave me a heart wound; By Gods blessing my old Foundation was broken up and I saw that my righteousness would not save me; then I was convinced of the doctrine of Election and went right to quarreling with God about it; because that all I could do would not save me; and he had decreed from Eternity who should be saved and who not... *

*William and Mary Quarterly, XXXIII, No. 1 (Jan. 1976) 2-3.

Lifelong Preaching

Whitefield returned to England in 1741 and found that although the revival was continuing, John Wesley was diverting from the Calvinistic doctrine that Whitefield preached. They parted company theologically, although they reconciled years later. Whitefield's friends built a large wooden church, Moorfields Tabernacle, for him to preach in whenever they could pull him inside. For 31 years Whitefield preached virtually every day in almost every place in the English-speaking world. He made 14 trips to Scotland (very successful), two trips to Ireland (where he was almost killed), and several trips to Wales, where in 1741 he met an older widow and married (not very successful).

Whitefield preached a schedule that would have destroyed even a healthy man, and Whitefield was far from healthy. He preached usually thirteen sermons a week, each lasting one to two hours or more. It is estimated that he preached 18,000 sermons in his lifetime. Even when he tried to rest, the crowds forced him to continue. What was the key to his remarkable ability to reach, hold, and change thousands of people every day?

Whitefield had a unique ability to paint pictures with words. Thousands of jeering, shoving, boisterous people would turn stone silent as soon as he started preaching. His voice was like that of a lion. Everyone heard and everyone understood, because he spoke common English using common stories. But almost like a hypnotist, he could build up a scene with such description and emotion that the entire congregation was in Heaven or Hell with him. One story that involved fighting a tempest at sea was so dramatic that an old sailor in the crowd started shouting, "Man the lifeboats!" even though they were all standing in a pasture. What a divine gift Whitefield had. No one since has matched his skills or his audiences.

Although thousands found faith and hope through Whitefield's work, he also had tormentors and enemies. He was jeered and ridiculed, pelted with stones and dead cats, and even attacked and beaten by a man with a gold-headed cane. Nothing deterred or even delayed his preaching. He was fearless in his work and frequently proclaimed, "We are immortal till our work is done." He was always joyful, generous, and accepting. When a Quaker chided him about wearing his full Anglican vestments, Whitefield replied that he should be allowed to wear his vestments if the Quaker was allowed to wear his peculiar hat.

Although a priest of the Anglican Church, his ministry cut across all denominations and sects. As he so clearly explained in a sermon from a courthouse balcony in 1740:

> "Father Abraham, whom have you in heaven? Any Episcopalians? No! Any Presbyterians? No! Any Independents or Methodists? No, no, no! Whom have you there? We don't know those names here. All who are here are Christians... Oh, is this the case? Then God help us to forget party names and to become Christians in deed and truth."

The Countess of Huntingdon appointed him as one of her chaplains and financed sixty-four Methodist meeting houses in England. He was instrumental in helping found the College of New Jersey (now Princeton University), the College of Philadelphia (now the University of Pennsylvania), and Dartmouth. He was a close friend to Benjamin Franklin, who was also his publisher in America. Franklin never converted to Christianity, but he admired and respected Whitefield and admitted that through Whitefield "it seemed as if the whole world was growing religious."

The Almost Husband

Whitefield frequently preached on being espoused to Christ, and that one had to devote their entire life and soul to being Christian. He also severely criticized people for being "almost Christians," those church-going, well-meaning, yet unconverted souls. His convictions were sincere, but after visiting Jonathon Edwards in New England and meeting his charming and devout wife, Whitefield decided he needed to marry. His first attempt was a letter to the parents of a young girl he had met in America. "I am free from the foolish passion that the world calls love. I write only because I believe it is the will of God that I should alter my state, but your denial will finally convince me that your daughter is not the person appointed for me." The parents, perhaps at the daughter's pleading, declined the offer. However, when Whitefield returned to England he learned of a widow in Wales, between the ages of thirty and forty (even 250 years ago, widows did not readily admit their ages), who was a "despised follower of the lamb." They were married in 1741 and had a child in 1743, but the son died at four months old. Whitefield made virtually no mention of his wife in his journals, and the kindest thing said about their marriage was that it was not a happy union. They were married for twenty-seven years, but Whitefield was rarely at home, and she did not travel with him. They were separated for years at a time, and when she died in 1768, it set his "mind at rest."

Called Home

Although suffering continually from asthma, Whitefield refused to give up his daily sermons. In 1769 he made his final trip to America, arriving in Savannah to work on converting his orphanage to a college. He traveled up the Atlantic coast with crowds at every stop. By the time he reached Boston, he was too ill to speak and spent three days in bed. On September 29, he was carried to Exeter, New Hampshire, where he prayed, "Lord Jesus, I am weary in your work, but not of your work. If I have not yet finished my course, let me go and speak for you once more in the fields, seal your truth, and come home to die." Barely able to stand, Whitefield preached for two hours on "Faith and Works," and then went to his friend's house in Newburyport for supper and bed. But when he tried to walk up the stairs to bed, dozens of people appeared at the parsonage and begged for just a short message. Whitefield stood on the steps and spoke until the candle he was holding in his hand burned down to his palm. He told a companion that his asthma was returning and, "I am dying." At 6:00 the next morning he died. He was 55 years old.

Whitefield's Legacy

Oh, to have a recording of Whitefield preaching! But, he lived two centuries too early. Although we have his written work, it does not begin to express the faith, emotion, and excitement that Whitefield produced every day of his life. As the great Baptist preacher, C. H. Spurgeon said, "He lived. Other men seemed to be only half-alive; but Whitefield was all life, fire, wing, force." Although ridiculed and ostracized by the Church of England during his lifetime, the Church did come to recognize what a powerful and true believer he was. In 1989 the Church founded the George Whitefield College as the official theological college of the Church of England in South Africa. Colleges, schools, and churches named after Whitefield were also founded in England and America.

Harvard University Library owes gratitude to Whitefield, for when their first library was destroyed by fire, Whitefield appealed to the people of England and they donated replacements for a whole new library. We even owe Whitefield gratitude for one of our favorite Christmas carols. Charles Wesley wrote, "Hark How All the Welkins Ring," but when Whitefield published the hymn, he thankfully changed the first line to, "Hark The Herald Angels Sing."

But more important than any school or library was the profound change that Whitefield made in the people of England and America. He was never interested in buildings or money. (He once had to sell his own furniture to pay for his mother's care, and he died a pauper.) He only cared about his mission. But historians note that Whitefield's evangelism also served another purpose in the colonies. Although never political and always English, Whitefield gave Americans a common belief and showed them how, if unified, they could successfully challenge any authority of the day—religious or political. Within a few months of his death, the first shots were fired in Boston, and Americans were on another road, the road to independence.

George Whitefield was not political or even interested in organizations or governments. His whole existence was for the saving of souls, every soul, in every known place. In a time when most people never traveled more than 30 miles from their birthplaces, George Whitefield sailed, rode, and walked thousands of miles for his Lord Jesus Christ. He didn't need a church, a denomination, or even a roof. With his traveling, foldable pulpit, his faith, and his magnificent voice, he was truly God's trumpet in the wilderness.

Sue E. Tennant

References

Christian Word, George Whitefield, www.christianword.org.

Christianity Today, *131 Christians Everyone Should Know*, www.christianitytoday.com

Eerdmans, William B. *Eerdmans' Handbook to Christianity in America*, William B. Eerdmans Publishing Company, 1983.

Hattersley, Roy, *The Life of John Wesley*, Random House, 2003.

Littlewood, David, *The Power Message of George Whitefield*, www.theremnant.com

Orentas, Dr. Rimas J. *George Whitefield: Lightening Rod of the Great Awakening* www.dylee.keel.econ.ship.edu.

The Anglican Library, *George Whitefield*, www.anglicanlibrary.org.

Truth for Today, *George Whitefield*, www.tecmalta.org.

SingleSpoon Ministries, *George Whitefield*, www.singlespoon.org.

Illustration Portfolio

REV. GEORGE WHITEFIELD

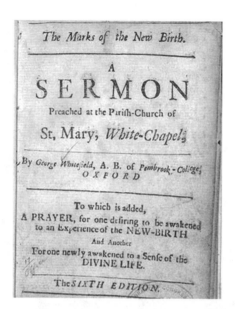

A WHITFIELD TRACT ON THE SUBJECT OF THE NEW BIRTH

THE WESLEY BROTHERS AND WHITEFIELD WERE MEMBERS OF THE
HOLY CLUB AT OXFORD.

John Wesley, John Fletcher and George Whitfield stayed at
the Trevecca Farmhouse when they went to open the
Trevecca College in 1768.

CHARLES WESLEY

JOHN WESLEY

WHITEFIELD BROKE WITH TRADITION BY PREACHING IN THE STREET.
OPEN AIR PREACHING WAS UNACCEPTABLE, UNDIGNIFIED, DIRTY
AND ILLEGAL.

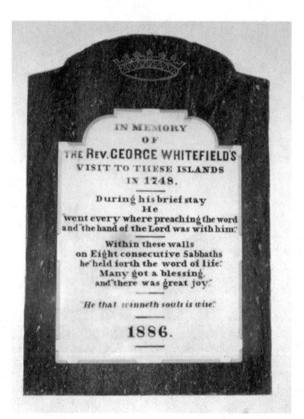

A MEMORIAL PLAQUE COMMEMORATING WHITEFIELD'S VISIT TO
BURMUDA IN 1748

LETTER I.

From the Rev. Mr. Whitefield,

at Georgia, *to a Friend in* London, *wherein he vindicates his Afferting*, That Archbishop *Tillotson* knew no more of true Christianity than *Mahomet*.

Savannah, January 18. 1739,40.

My Dear Friend,

THO' that Saying of the Psalmist, *Thou shalt answer for me, O Lord my God*, has generally been a Rule for my Conduct, in respect to my Adversaries; yet when the Glory of God, and the Welfare of his People are concern'd, I think it my Duty to maintain whatever I have afferted in any of my Discourses, either publick or private.---My affirming *That Archbishop* Tillotson *knew no more of Christianity than* Mahomet, has been look'd upon as one of the most unjustifiable Expressions that ever proceeded out of my Mouth: For this I am not only look'd upon as a greater Monster than ever by my Enemies, but also have been secretly despised and censured by some, who, otherwise, were my Friends. Indeed, I dare not say this Expression came originally from me: No; my dear and honoured Friend Mr. *John Wesly*, if I mistake not, first spoke it in a private Society, when he was expounding Part of St. *Paul's* Epistle to the *Romans*, and proving the Doctrine of Justification in the Sight of God, by Faith alone, in Contradistinction to good Works. It is in this particular (not to mention others) that I have and do now join Issue with my honour'd Friend, and upon the maturest Deliberation, say again what I have often said

BENJAMIN FRANKLIN PUBLISHED THIS LETTER WRITTEN TO HIM BY GEORGE WHITEFIELD.

WHITEFIELD WAS CHRISTENED AT ST. MARY DE CRYPT (RIGHT).
IN 1736, HE PREACHED HIS FIRST SERMON THERE.

THE BELL INN, WHITEFIELD'S BIRTHPLACE, AS IT APPEARS TODAY.

A Memorial Plaque at the site of Tottenham-Court Chapel,
at Bunhill Fields, built by Whitefield in 1756.
The chapel was nicknamed "the soul trap."

The Whitefield Cenotaph in Newbury, Massachusetts

Whitefield's Beginning as an Open Air Preacher

When the Anglican Church chased Whitefield out of London, he decided to visit Bristol until the excitement subsided. He selected Bristol because of the sharp remark of an acquaintance who said, "You went to America to convert the Indians. If you have a mind to convert the Indians, what about the coalminers of Kingswood, who are without spiritual care?" Whitefield found conditions in Bristol worse than he had imagined. There were whole families in the Kingswood colliery district who had never seen a Bible, had never stepped foot within a church and who had never heard the name of the Savior except in profanity. The local churches appeared to be totally indifferent to the spiritual needs of this district. Whitefield, as an obedient clergyman of the Established Church, went to the chancellor of the diocese, who informed him bluntly that he was forbidden to preach in that diocese without a license. The canons prohibited it. The quick-witted Whitefield replied that the same canons prohibited ordained clergymen from hanging about in the public houses, drinking and playing at cards.

Whitefield made no further attempt to preach in the churches. He went promptly to St. Nicholas Street and started to preach. A great crowd collected. Then, on February 17, 1739, he took his stand on a hill on the outskirts of Bristol, in Kingswood Common, and preached to a congregation of 200. His next sermon drew 3,000 people. The third sermon attracted 5,000 and in a short time he was preaching to congregations of 20,000. In graphic words he describes the miners, many of whom had never before listened to a sermon, standing before him with their tears cutting white furrows through the coal dust on their faces. "The open firmament above me," he wrote, "the prospect of the adjacent fields, with the sight of thousands and thousands, some in coaches, some on horseback, and some in the trees, and at all times affected and drenched in tears together, to which sometimes was added the solemnity of the approaching evening, was almost too much for and quite overcame me."

(Webber, F. R., *A History of Preaching in Britain and America*, Vol. 1, pp. 354-55.)

This can be both an encouragement and a great discouragement. If we leave the help of God out of the equation for a moment, I must say, after preaching open air thousands of times, that it's not as easy to draw a crowd nowadays. We live in an entertainment age, where if there's not a car chase within two minutes, it's boring. So, people aren't drawn so easily to someone on a soapbox as they have been in the past. We will look at how to draw and hold a crowd, later on in this publication. — *Ray Comfort*

First Thoughts of Preaching Open Air

Accordingly, after knowing that a host of people had stood outside a church while he had preached within, he said, "This put me first upon thinking of preaching without doors. I mentioned it to some friends who looked upon it as a mad notion. However, we kneeled down and prayed that nothing may be done rashly."

Whitefield's Work Ethic

Had I a hundred hands, I could employ them all. The harvest is very great. I am ashamed I can do no more for Him who has done so much for me.

(Tyerman, Vol. 1, p. 273.)

How Whitefield puts into words how each of us should feel about the gift of life and for the love expressed at the cross. His motivation to reach the lost was fueled by an unending gratitude, and gratitude of those who see the cross can't easily be put into words. — Ray Comfort

The Joy of Preaching Christ

Preached this morning in Moorfields to about twenty thousand people, who were very quiet and attentive, and much affected. Went to public worship morning and evening, and at six preached at Kennington. Such a sight I never saw before. I believe there were no less than fifty thousand people, and near four score coaches, besides great numbers of horses. God gave me great enlargement of heart. I continued my discourse for an hour and a half, and when I returned home I was filled with such love, peace and joy that I cannot express it.

(Excerpt from: *George Whitefield—God's Anointed Servant in the Great Revival of the Eighteenth Century*, p. 52.)

Pleasing God

I believe I was never more acceptable to my Master than when I was standing to teach those hearers in the open fields. Some may censure me; but if I thus pleased men, I should not be the servant of Christ.

(Tyerman, Vol. 1, p.180.)

I want to shout, "Amen" to this. We are never so much in the will of God as when we are doing exactly what He tells us to do. — Ray Comfort

Results of Early Opposition

I never was more opposed and never met with so great success. I hope I shall learn more and more every day, that no place is amiss for preaching the Gospel. God forbid that the Word of God should be bound because some deny the use of their churches! The more I am bid to hold my peace, the more earnestly will I lift up my voice like a trumpet, and tell the people what must be done in them before they can be finally saved by Jesus Christ.

(From Whitefield's Journal, quoted in Tyerman, Vol. 1, p. 175.)

Whitefield's Work Ethic

Had I a hundred hands, I could employ them all. The harvest is very great. I am ashamed I can do no more for Him who has done so much for me.

(Tyerman, Vol. 1, p. 273.)

How Whitefield puts into words how each of us should feel about the gift of life, and for the love expressed at the cross. His motivation to reach the lost was fueled by an unending gratitude, and gratitude of those who see the cross can't easily be put into words. — Ray Comfort

Whitefield Encourages a New Open Air Preacher

L et the love of Jesus constrain you to go out into the highways and hedges to compel poor sinners to come in. Some may say, "This is not proceeding with a zeal according to knowledge;" but I am persuaded, when the power of religion revives, the gospel must be propagated in the same manner as it was first established, by itinerant preaching. Go on, dear sir, go on and follow your glorious Master without the camp, bearing His reproach. Never fear the scourge of the tongue, or the threatenings that are daily breathed out against the Lord, and against His Christ. Suffer we must. Ere long perhaps, we may sing in a prison, and have our feet in the stocks; but faith in Jesus turns a prison into a palace, and makes a bed of flames become a bed of down [roses]. Let us be faithful today, and our Lord will support us tomorrow.

(Whitefield's letter to Rev. George Stonehouse, cited in Tyerman, Vol. 1, p. 393.)

Child Evangelism

I think I never was so drawn out to pray for little children, and invite them to Jesus Christ. I had just heard of a child, who, after hearing me preach, was immediately taken sick, and said, "I will go to Mr. Whitefield's God." In a short time he died. This encouraged me to speak to little ones; but oh, how were the old people affected, when I said, "Little children, if your parents will not come to Christ, do you come, and go to Heaven without them." There seemed to be but few dry eyes. I have not seen a greater commotion during my preaching at Boston.

(Tyerman, Vol. 1, p. 417.)

Unconverted Ministers

The Lord enabled me to open my mouth boldly against unconverted ministers;[13] for, I am persuaded, the generality of preachers talk of an unknown and unfelt Christ. The reason why congregations have been so dead is because they have had dead men preaching to them. O that the Lord may quicken and revive them! How can dead men beget living children?

(Tyerman, Vol. 1, p. 417.)

Unconverted ministers are the bane of the Christian church.

(Tyerman, Vol. 1, p. 428.)

In these days, in which there is a lack of understating the biblical reality of false converts, the words "unconverted minister" seem to be an oxymoron. ━ _Ray Comfort_

The Name of George Whitefield

I care not if the name of George Whitefield be banished out of the world, so that Jesus be exalted in it. (Whitefield, in a letter to a minister in Wales.

Quoted in Tyerman, Vol. 2, p. 33.)

Whitefield Hit With a Rock

The day after I wrote your ladyship, I preached twice at Exeter, and, in the evening, I believe I had near ten thousand hearers. The bishop and several of his clergy stood very near me, as I am informed. A good season it was. All was quiet, and there was a great solemnity in the congregation; but a drunken man threw at me three great stones. One of them cut my head deeply, and was likely to knock me off the table; but blessed be God! I was not at all discomposed.

(Whitefield's letter to Lady Huntingdon cited in Tyerman, Vol. 2, p. 232.)

Advice to Preachers

There is nothing like keeping the wheels oiled by action. The more we do, the more we may do; every act strengthens the habit; and the best preparation for preaching on Sundays is to preach every day of the week.

(Whitefield's letter to an Oxford Methodist cited in Tyerman, Vol. 2, p. 260.)

A Letter to Benjamin Franklin

I find that you grow more and more famous in the learned world. As you have made a pretty considerable progress in the mysteries of electricity, I would now humbly recommend to your diligent unprejudiced pursuit and study the mystery of the new birth. It is a most important, interesting study, and, when mastered, will richly repay you for all your pains. One, at whose bar we are shortly to appear, has solemnly declared that, without it, "We cannot enter into the kingdom of heaven."

(Tyerman, Vol. 2, p. 283.)

Whitefield's Preference for the Open Air

London cares and London labors, I expect, will bring me low again; but I hope soon to slip away, and to get strength, and then to hunt for precious souls again. How gladly would I bid adieu to ceiled houses, and vaulted roofs! Mounts are the best pulpits, and the heavens the best sounding boards. O for power equal to my will! I would fly from pole to pole, publishing the everlasting Gospel of the Son of God.

(Tyerman, Vol. 2, p. 453.)

Whitefield's Faith in God

Come," said Whitefield to his friend and host, Andrew Kinsman, "come, let us go to some of the poor and afflicted of your flock. It is not enough that we labor in the pulpit; we must endeavor to be useful out of it." Away the two friends went, and Whitefield not only gave counsel to those they visited, but monetary aid. Kinsman reminded him that his finances were low, and that he was more bountiful than he could afford. "Young man," replied Whitefield, "it is not enough to pray, and to put on a serious countenance: pure religion and undefiled is this, to visit the fatherless and widows in their affliction and to administer to their wants. My stock, I grant, is nearly exhausted, but God will soon send me a fresh supply." In the evening, a gentleman called, and asked to see Whitefield. "Sir," said he, "I heard you preach yesterday: you are on a journey, as well as myself; and, as traveling is expensive, will you do me the honor of accepting this?" The present was five guineas and came from a man noted for his penuriousness. "Young man," cried Whitefield, on his return to Kinsman, "young man, God has soon repaid what I bestowed. Learn in future, not to withhold when it is in the power of your hand to give."

(Tyerman, Vol. 2, p. 456.)

The Greatest Job Under Heaven

The greatest preferment under heaven is to be an able, painful, faithful, successful, suffering, cast-out minister of the New Testament.

(Tyerman, Vol. 2, p. 509.)

Field Preaching Forever

It is good to go into the highways and hedges. Field preaching, field preaching forever!

(Tyerman, Vol. 2, p. 560.)

※·※◎※·※

Come Down, Rebels

It is said that when once preaching in a graveyard, two young men conducted themselves improperly, when he fixed his eyes upon them, and with a voice resembling thunder, said, "Come down, you rebels." They instantly fell, neither of them being inclined again to come into contact with such a look, or to hear such a voice.

(Belcher, Joseph, *George Whitefield: A Biography*, pp. 465-66.)

Open air preaching is nothing like preaching within a church building. Neither is it like personal witnessing. If you listened to me share the Gospel with one or two people, you would probably notice an obvious gentleness in my tone. However, if you listen to me preach in the open air, it might sometimes seem a little contentious and provocative. If I preached the same way I speak in a church or one-on-one, I will never hold a crowd.

It is important in both cases that I am motivated by love, but if I don't keep the preaching "on the edge," I will lose my hearers in minutes (if not seconds).

John Wesley put it this way: "In the streets a man must from beginning to end be intense, and for that very reason he must be condensed and concentrated in his thought and utterance."

This "intense" preaching may be misunderstood by those who don't know why it's there. The problem is that when we read the Gospels, we don't see the passion involved in discourses. When Jesus spoke, there were those in the crowd that wanted to kill Him. They hated Him. People no doubt called out, accusing Him of blasphemy or asking Him questions. Without question, the atmosphere would have been electric. That's the atmosphere that holds a crowd's attention.

To become passive in the name of love and gentleness will pull the plug out and the electricity will immediately leave. If you do this, be ready to be accused of preaching without love. The accusations almost always come for those brethren who have never preached in the open air.
When speaking of open air preaching, R. A. Torrey said, "Don't be soft. One of these nice, namby-pamby, sentimental sort of fellows in an open-air meeting the crowd cannot and will not stand. The temptation to throw a brick or a rotten apple at him is perfectly irresistible, and one can hardly blame the crowd." — Ray Comfort

Stirred to Preach Open Air

T he Baptists of the Southern Colonies in particular benefited from Whitefield's influence. Baptist churches and Baptist people were few in the South at the time, unbelief was entering among them, and a zeal for soul-winning was rare. But moved by Whitefield's ministry many of these churches became firm in the faith, and a new fervor began to characterize them. They increased in number with great speed as men—many of them farmer-preachers—preached the gospel in tents, in barns, and in the open air. Souls in great numbers were won to Christ.

(Excerpt from: *George Whitefield – God's Anointed Servant in the Great Revival of the Eighteenth Century*, p. 86.)

Is your heart becoming stirred to preach open air? Is your concern for the lost beginning to overcome your fears? Don't ignore that conviction. You are needed. Don't confess your weakness. Instead say to yourself, "I can do all things through Christ who strengthens me." Go to our Boot Camp. It's life-changing. — Ray Comfort

Eternal Punishment

S urely; God will not be so cruel as to damn you only for eating an apple, it cannot be." Alas! How many does Satan lead captive at his will, by flattering them, that they shall not surely die; that Hell torments will not be eternal; that God is all mercy; that He therefore will not punish a few years sin with an eternity of misery? But Eve found God as good as His word; and so will all they who go on in sin, under a false hope that they shall not surely die.

(Whitefield, George "The Seed of the Woman, and the Seed of the Serpent")

Law in Evangelism

"What is this that you have done?" God would here awaken her to a sense of her crime and danger, and therefore, as it were, thunders in her ears: for the Law must be preached to self-righteous sinners. Secure sinners must hear the thunderings of Mount Sinai, before we bring them to Mount Zion. They, who never preach up the Law, it is to be feared, are unskillful in delivering the glad tidings of the gospel. Every minister should be a Boanerges, a son of thunder, as well as a Barnabus, a son of consolation. There was an earthquake and a whirlwind, before the small still voice came to Elijah. We must first show people they are condemned, and then show them how they must be saved. But how and when to preach the Law, and when to apply the promises of the gospel, wisdom is profitable to direct. "And the Lord God said unto the woman, 'What is this that you have done?'"

("The Seed of the Woman …")

Open Air Preaching

To confine our communion within church-walls, and to think that Jesus could not preach in a field as well as on consecrated ground; this is Judaism, this is bigotry: this is like Peter, who would not go to preach the gospel to the Gentiles, till he had a vision from God: and when his conduct was blamed by the disciples, he could not satisfy them till he had acquainted them with the vision he had seen.

("… Being Not Righteous Enough")

Self Righteousness

If I had a voice so great, and could speak so loud, as that the whole world could hear me, I would cry, "Be not righteous over-much," by bringing your righteousness to Christ, and by being righteous in your own eyes. Man must be abased, that God may be exalted.

("...Being Not Righteous Enough.")

Self Deception

Do not think you are Christians; do not flatter yourselves with being righteous enough, and good enough, because you lead moral decent lives, do no one any harm, go to church, and attend upon the outward means of grace; no, my brethren, you may do this, and a great deal more, and yet be very far from having a saving, experimental knowledge of Jesus Christ.

("...Being Not Righteous Enough.")

Addressing False Accusations

O that some sinner might be brought to Jesus Christ! Do not say I preach despair; I despair of no one, when I consider God had mercy on such a wretch as I, who was running in a full career to Hell. I was hastening thither, but Jesus Christ passed by and stopped me; Jesus Christ passed by me while I was in my blood, when I was polluted with filth; He passed by me, and bid me live. Thus I am a monument of God's free grace; and therefore, my brethren, I despair of none of you, when I consider, I say, what a wretch I was. I am not speaking now out of a false humility, a pretended sanctity, as the Pharisees call it: no, the truth in Christ I speak, and therefore, men and devils do your worst. I have a gracious Master who will protect me; it is His work I am engaged in, and Jesus Christ will carry me above their rage.

("...Being Not Righteous Enough.")

Plea to Sinners

Can you bear to think of a bleeding, panting, dying Jesus, offering Himself up for sinners, and you will not accept Him? Do not say, you are poor, and therefore are ashamed to go to church, for God has sent the gospel out to you. Do not harden your hearts: oppose not the will of Jesus.

("...Being Not Righteous Enough.")

The Reality of Judgment

My dear friends, I would preach with all my heart till midnight, to do you good, till I could preach no more. O that this body might hold out to speak more for my dear Redeemer! Had I a thousand lives, had I a thousand tongues, they should be employed in inviting sinners to come to Jesus Christ! Come, then, let me prevail with some of you to come along with me. Come, poor, lost, undone sinner, come just as you are to Christ, and say, If I be damned, I will perish at the feet of Jesus Christ, where never one perished yet. He will receive you with open arms; the dear Redeemer is willing to receive you all. Fly, then, for your lives. The devil is in you while unconverted; and will you go with the devil in your heart to bed this night? God Almighty knows if ever you and I shall see one another again. In one or two days I must go, and, perhaps, I may never see you again till I meet you at the Judgment Day. O my dear friends, think of that solemn meeting; think of that important hour, when the heavens shall pass away with fervent heat, when the sea and the grave shall be giving up their dead, and all shall be summoned to their great God.

(Whitefield "The Kingdom of God", cited in Dargan, Edwin Charles, *A History Of Preaching*, Vol. 2, p. 314.)

The Word of God

If we once get above our Bibles, and cease making the written word of God our sole rule both as to faith and practice, we shall soon lie open to all manner of delusion, and be in great danger of making shipwreck of faith and a good conscience. Our blessed Lord, though He had the Spirit of God without measure, yet always was governed by, and fought the devil with, "It is written."

("Walking with God")

Prayer

The spirit of grace is always accompanied with the spirit of supplication. It is the very breath of the new creature, the fan of the divine life, whereby the spark of holy fire, kindled in the soul by God, is not only kept in, but raised into a flame.

("Walking with God")

Stop!

Stop, stop, O sinner! Turn, turn, O you unconverted men, for the end of that way you are now walking in, however right it may seem in your blinded eyes, will be death, even eternal destruction both of body and soul. Make no longer tarrying, I say: At your peril I charge you, step not one step further on in your present walk. For how do you know, O man, but the next step you take may be into Hell? Death may seize you, judgment find you, and then the great gulf will be fixed between you and endless glory forever and ever.

("Walking with God")

The Danger of a False Convert

An almost Christian is one of the most hurtful creatures in the world. He is a wolf in sheep's clothing. He is one of those false prophets, of whom our blessed Lord bids us beware, who would persuade men that the way to Heaven is broader than it really is; and, thereby, enter not into the kingdom of God themselves, and those that are entering in they hinder. These, these are the men who turn the world into a lukewarm, Laodicean spirit; who hang out false lights, and so shipwreck unthinking benighted souls in their voyage to the haven where they would be. These are they that are greater enemies to the cross of Christ than infidels themselves; for, of an unbeliever everyone will be aware; but an almost Christian, through his subtle hypocrisy, draws many after him, and therefore must expect to receive the greater condemnation.

("The Almost Christian," quoted in Tyerman, Rev. L., *The Life of the Rev. George Whitefield,* Vol. 1, p. 96.)

Fools for Christ

O that Christless sinners knew what it is to have fellowship with the Father and the Son! They would envy the happiness of saints, and count it all joy to be termed enthusiasts and fools for Christ's sake.

("Abraham's Offering Up His Son Isaac")

Unreasonable Sinners

We have sufficient testimony that God has spoken to us by His Son; why should we not also believe, though many things in the New Testament are above our reason?

For, where reason ends, faith begins. And, however infidels may style themselves reasoners, of all men they are the most unreasonable. For, is it not contrary to all reason, to measure an infinite by a finite understanding, or think to find out the mysteries of godliness to perfection?

("Abraham's Offering...")

All we ask of our hearers is that they be open to reason. There are not many witnessing and preaching encounters as frustrating as an unreasonable sinner (one who hears simple common sense, and yet discards it as unworthy of consideration). — Ray Comfort

Morning Devotions

It is often remarked of people in the Old Testament, that they rose early in the morning; and particularly of our Lord in the New, that He rose a great while before day to pray. The morning befriends devotion; and, if people cannot use so much self-denial as to rise early to pray, I know not how they will be able to die at a stake (if called to it) for Jesus Christ.

("Abraham's Offering...")

The Cross

Look by faith, behold the blessed Jesus, our all-glorious Emmanuel, not bound, but nailed on an accursed tree. See how He hangs crowned with thorns, and in derision of all that are round about Him: see how the thorns pierce Him, and how the blood in purple streams trickle down His sacred temples! Hark how the God of nature groans! See how He bows His head, and at length humanity gives up the ghost! Isaac is saved, but Jesus, the God of Isaac, dies. A ram is offered up in Isaac's room, but Jesus has no substitute; Jesus must bleed, Jesus must die. God the Father provided this Lamb for Himself from all eternity. He must be offered in time, or man must be damned for evermore. And now, where are your tears? Shall I say, Refrain your voice from weeping? No, rather let me exhort you to look to Him whom you have pierced, and mourn, as a woman mourns for her first-born: for we have been the betrayers, we have been the murderers of this Lord of glory; and shall we not bewail those sins, which brought the blessed Jesus to the accursed tree? Having so much done, so much suffered for us, so much forgiven, shall we not love much! O! let us love Him with all our hearts, and minds, and strength, and glorify Him in our souls and bodies, for they are His. Which leads me to a second inference I shall draw from the foregoing discourse.

("Abraham's Offering…")

Family Devotions

Was a minister to disregard teaching his people publicly, and from house to house, and to excuse himself by saying, that he had enough to do to work out his own salvation with fear and trembling, without concerning himself with that of others; would you not be apt to think such a minister, to be like the unjust judge, "One that neither feared God, nor regarded man?" And yet, odious as such a character would be, it is no worse than that governor of a family deserves, who thinks himself obliged only to have his own soul, without paying any regard to the souls of his household. For every house is as it were a parish, and every master is concerned to secure, as much as in him lies, the spiritual prosperity of every one under his roof, as any minister whatever is obliged to look to the spiritual welfare of every individual person under his charge.

("The Great Duty of Family Religion")

Judgment Day for Parents

R emember, the time will come, and that perhaps very shortly, when we must all appear before the judgment-seat of Christ; where we must give a solemn and strict account how we have had our conversation, in our respective families in this world. How will you endure to see your children and servants (who ought to be your joy and crown of rejoicing in the day of our Lord Jesus Christ) coming out as so many swift witnesses against you; cursing the father that begot them, the womb that bore them, the breasts they have sucked, and the day they ever entered into your houses? Think you not, the damnation which men must endure for their own sins, will be sufficient, that they need load themselves with the additional guilt of being accessory to the damnation of others also? O consider this, all ye that forget to serve the Lord with your respective households, "lest he pluck you away, and there be none to deliver you!"

("The Great Duty of Family Religion")

The Third Commandment

A sk the drunkard why he rises up early to follow strong drink, and he will tell you, because it affords his sensual appetite some kind of pleasure and gratification, though it be no higher than that of a brute. Inquire of the covetous worldling why he defrauds and over-reaches his neighbor, and he has an answer ready: to enrich himself and lay up goods for many years. But it must certainly puzzle the profane swearer himself, to inform you what pleasure he reaps from swearing: for alas! it is a fruitless tasteless thing that he sells his soul for. But indeed he does not sell it at all: in this case he prodigally gives it away (without repentance) to the devil; and parts with a blessed eternity, and runs into everlasting torment, merely for nothing.

("The Heinous Sin of Profane Cursing and Swearing")

Blasphemy in Hell

T he damned devils, and damned souls of men in hell, may be supposed to rave and blaspheme in their torments, because they know that the chains wherein they are held, can never be knocked off; but for men that swim in the river of God's goodness, whose mercies are renewed to them every morning, and who are visited with fresh tokens of his infinite unmerited loving-kindness every moment; for these favorite creatures to set their mouths against heaven, and to blaspheme a gracious, patient, all-bountiful God; is a height of sin which exceeds the blackness and impiety of devils and hell itself.

("The Heinous Sin of Profane Cursing and Swearing")

He Will Not Hold Them Guiltless

For what can be more base, than one hour to pretend to adore God in public worship, and the very next moment to blaspheme His name; indeed, such a behavior, from persons who deny the being of a God, (if any such fools there be) is not altogether too much to be wondered at; but for men, who not only subscribe to the belief of a Deity, but likewise acknowledge him to be a God of infinite majesty and power. For such men to blaspheme His holy name, by profane cursing and swearing, and at the same time confess, that this very God has expressly declared, He will not hold him guiltless, but will certainly and eternally punish (without repentance) him that takes His name in vain; is such an instance of fool-hardiness, as well as baseness, that can scarcely be paralleled. This is what they presume not to do in other cases of less danger: they dare not revile a general at the head of his army, nor rouse a sleeping lion when within reach of his paw. And is the Almighty God, the great Jehovah, the everlasting King, who can consume them by the breath of his nostrils, and frown them to Hell in an instant; is He the only contemptible being in their account that may be provoked without fear, and offended without punishment? No; though God hear long, He will not bear always; the time will come, and that too, perhaps, much sooner than such persons may expect, when God will vindicate His injured honor, when He will lay bare His almighty arm, and make those wretches feel the eternal smart of His justice, show power and name they have so often vilified and blasphemed. Alas! what will become of all their bravery then? Will they then wantonly sport with the name of their Maker, and call upon the King of all the earth to damn them any more in jest? No, their note will then be changed: indeed, they shall call, but it will be for "the rocks to fall on them, and the hills to cover them from the wrath of Him that sits upon the throne, and from the Lamb forever." It is true; there was a time when they prayed, though perhaps without thought, for damnation both for themselves and others. And now they will find their prayers answered.

("The Heinous Sin of Profane Cursing and Swearing")

The Rich Young Ruler

For our Lord, by referring him to the commandments, did not (as the objectors insinuate) in the least hint, that his morality would recommend him to the favor and mercy of God; but he intended thereby, to make the Law his schoolmaster to bring him to himself; that the young man, seeing how he had broken every one of these Commandments, might thereby be convinced of the insufficiency of his own, and consequently of the absolute necessity of looking out for a better righteousness, whereon he might depend for eternal life. This was what our Lord designed. The young man being self-righteous, and willing to justify himself, said, "All these have I observed from my youth;" but had he known himself, he would have confessed, all these have I broken from my youth. For, supposing he had not actually committed adultery, had he never lusted after a woman in his heart? What, if he had not really killed another, had he never been angry without a cause, or spoken unadvisedly with his lips? If so, by breaking one of the least Commandments in the least degree, he became liable to the curse of God: for "cursed is he (saith the Law) that continues not to do all things that are written in this book." And therefore, as observed before, our Lord was so far from speaking against, that He treated the young man in that manner, on purpose to convince him of the necessity of an imputed righteousness.

("The Lord Our Righteousness")

Gratitude

My brethren, my heart is enlarged towards you! O think of the love of Christ in dying for you! If the Lord is your righteousness, let the righteousness of your Lord be continually in your mouth. Talk of, O talk of, and recommend the righteousness of Christ, when you lie down, and when you rise up, at your going out and coming in! Think of the greatness of the gift, as well as the giver! Show to all the world, in whom you have believed! Let all by your fruits know, that the Lord is your righteousness, and that you are waiting for your Lord from Heaven! O study to be holy, even as He who has called you, and washed you in His own blood, is holy! Let not the righteousness of the Lord be evil spoken of through you. Let not Jesus be wounded in the house of His friends, but grow in grace, and in the knowledge of our Lord and Savior Jesus Christ, day by day. O think of His dying love! Let that love constrain you to obedience! Having much forgiven, love much. Be always asking, What shall I do to express my gratitude to the Lord for giving me His righteousness? Let that self-abasing, God-exalting question be always in your mouths; "Why me, Lord? Why me?" why am I taken, and others left? Why is the Lord my righteousness? Why is He become my salvation, who has so often deserved damnation at His hands?

("The Lord Our Righteousness")

Distress for Sinners

O Christless sinners, I am distressed for you! The desires of my soul are enlarged. O that this may be an accepted time! That the Lord may be your righteousness! For where would you flee if death should find you naked? Indeed there is no hiding yourselves from His presence. The pitiful fig leaves of your own righteousness will not cover your nakedness, when God shall call you to stand before Him. Adam found them ineffectual, and so will you. O think of death! O think of judgment! Yet a little while, time will run out; and then what will become of you if the Lord is not your righteousness? Do you think that Christ will spare you? No, He who formed you will have no mercy on you. If you are not of Christ and if Christ is not your righteousness, Christ Himself shall pronounce you damned. And can you bear to think of being damned by Christ? Can you bear to hear the Lord Jesus say to you, "Depart from me, you cursed, into everlasting fire, prepared for the devil and his angels." Do you think you can live in everlasting burnings? Is your flesh brass, and are your bones iron? What if they are? Hell-fire, that fire prepared for the devil and his angels, will heat them through and through. And can you bear to depart from Christ? O that heart-piercing thought! Ask those holy souls who are at any time bewailing an absent God, who walk in darkness and see no light except for a few days or hours. Ask them what it is to lose a light and presence of Christ? See how they seek Him sorrowing, and go mourning after Him all the day long! And, if it is so dreadful to lose the sensible presence of Christ only for a day, what must it be to be banished from Him for all eternity!

("The Lord Our Righteousness")

Inviting Sinners to Repent

Knowing therefore the terrors of the Lord, let me persuade you to close with Christ, and never rest till you can say, "the Lord our righteousness." Who knows but the Lord may have mercy and abundantly pardon you? Beg of God to give you faith; and, if the Lord gives you that, you will by it receive Christ with His righteousness and His All. You need not fear the greatness or number of your sins. For are you sinners? So am I. Are you the chief of sinners? So am I. Are you backsliding sinners? So am I. And yet the Lord (forever adored be His rich, free and sovereign grace), the Lord is my righteousness. Come then, O young man, who (as I acted once myself) is playing the prodigal, and wandering away far away from your heavenly Father's house. Come home. Come home and leave your swine's trough. Feed no longer on the husks of sensual delights. For Christ's sake arise and come home! Your heavenly Father now calls you. See yonder the best robe, even the righteousness of His dear Son, awaits you. See it. View it again and again. Consider at how dear a rate it was purchased, even by the blood of God. Consider what great need you have of it. You are lost, undone, damned forever without it.

("The Lord Our Righteousness")

Covetousness

He took our Lord up into an exceeding high mountain, and showed him all the kingdoms of the world and the glory of them." He cares not how high he exalts us, or how high he is obliged to bid, so he can but get our hearts divided between God and the world. All this will he offer to give us, if we will only fall down and worship him. Arm us, dear Lord Jesus, with your Spirit, and help us under all such circumstances, to learn of you, and say unto the tempter, "Get thee hence, Satan; for it is written, you shall worship the Lord your God, and him only shall you serve.

("The Temptation of Christ")

Answering Those Who Sell the Conscience

B ut woe unto you that laugh now; for you shall then lament and weep." Woe unto you, who either believes there is no devil, or never felt any of his temptations. Woe unto you that are at ease in Zion, and instead of staying to be tempted by the devil, by idleness, self-indulgence, and making continual provision for the flesh, even tempt the devil to tempt you. Woe unto you, who not content with sinning yourselves, turn factors for Hell, and make a trade of tempting others to sin. Woe unto you, who either deny divine revelation, or never make use of it but to serve a bad turn. Woe unto you, who sell your consciences, and pawn your souls for a little worldly wealth or honor. Woe unto you, who climb up to high places, when in church or state, by corruption, bribery, extortion, cringing, flattery, or bowing down to, and soothing the vices of those by whom you expect to rise. Woe unto you! For whether you will own the relation or not, surely you are of your father the devil; for the works of your father you will do; I tremble for you. How can you escape the damnation of hell?

("The Temptation of Christ")

The greatest way to appeal to a sinner's conscience is to open up the Ten Commandments as Jesus did. Say, "This is what I am saying, 'God has appointed a Day in which He will judge the world in righteousness ... and that standard of judgment will be the Ten Commandments. Have you kept Commandments? Have you ever lied, stolen, lusted and therefore committed adultery in your heart? Jesus said, 'Whoever looks upon a woman to lust after her has committed adultery already with her in his heart.'"

Open up the Law. Preach the fact of the Judgment, the reality of Hell, the Cross, repentance, and faith. If you are open air preaching and hecklers are objecting, go back to crossing swords with your hearers, and don't be embarrassed to repeat the message again and again. Some will be new to the crowd, some not.

Sinners are dull of hearing, so it won't hurt them to hear it again. The great Puritan, Richard Baxter, said, "Screw the truth into men's minds." — Ray Comfort

Forgiveness

Thus you see how pleased the Lord Jesus Christ is with His spouse; and will not you, therefore, be espoused unto the Lord Jesus? I offer Jesus Christ to all of you; if you have been never so notorious for sin, if you have been as great a harlot as Mary Magdalen was, when once you are espoused to Christ, you shall be forgiven. Therefore, be not discouraged, at whatever slights and contempt the world may pass upon you, but come and join yourselves to the Lord Jesus Christ, and all your sins shall be washed away in His blood; and when once you are espoused to Jesus, you are disjoined from sin, you are born again.

("Christ, the Best Husband")

⁂

Refusing Christ

It is likewise your folly to refuse and neglect the gracious proffers of being the spouse of Christ. Hereby you forfeit all that love which He would bestow upon you. Hereby you choose rags before robes, dross before gold, pebbles before jewels, guilt before a pardon, wounds before healing, defilement before cleansing, deformity before comeliness, trouble before peace, slavery before liberty, the service of the devil before the service of Christ. Hereby you choose dishonor before a crown, death before life, Hell before Heaven, eternal misery and torment before everlasting joy and glory.

("Christ, the Best Husband")

⁂

The Incomparable Christ

Do you desire one that is great? He is of the highest dignity, He is the glory of heaven, the darling of eternity, admired by angels, dreaded by devils, and adored by saints. For you to be espoused to so great a king, what honor will you have by this espousal? Do you desire one that is rich? None is comparable to Christ; the fullness of the earth belongs to Him. If you are espoused to Christ, you shall share in His unsearchable riches; you shall receive of His fullness, even grace for grace here, and you shall hereafter be admitted to glory, and shall live with this Jesus to all eternity. Do you desire one that is wise? There is none comparable to Christ for wisdom. His knowledge is infinite, and His wisdom is correspondent thereto. And if you are espoused to Christ, He will guide and counsel you, and make you wise unto salvation. Do you desire one that is potent, who may defend you against your enemies, and all the insults and reproaches of the Pharisees of this generation? There is none that can equal Christ in power, for the Lord Jesus Christ has all power. Do you desire one that is good? There is none like unto Christ in this regard; others may have some goodness, but it is imperfect; Christ's goodness is complete and perfect, He is full of goodness and in Him dwells no evil. Do you desire one that is beautiful? His eyes are most sparkling. His looks and glances of love are ravishing. His smiles are most delightful and refreshing unto the soul. Christ is the most lovely person in the world. Do you desire one that can love you? None can love you like Christ; His love, my dear sisters, is incomprehensible. His love passes all other loves. The love of the Lord Jesus is first, without beginning; His love is free without any motive; His love is great without any measure; His love is constant without any change, and His love is everlasting.

("Christ, the Best Husband")

Espoused to Christ

But if any of you should ask, what you must do that you may be espoused unto Christ? You must be sensible of your need of being espoused to Him, and until you are sensible of your need of the Lord Jesus Christ, you cannot be espoused to Him. You must have desires after this Jesus, and seek unto Him for an interest in Him. You must cry nightly unto Him to espouse you to Himself. Put off the filthiness of sin and all its defilements; and then, my sisters, put on the white raiment, and clean garments, which Christ has provided for you, the robes of His righteousness. In these garments you shall be beautiful; and in these garments you shall be accepted: you must have the wedding garment on; you must put off all your own good works, for they will be but a means to keep you from Christ. No, you must come as not having your own righteousness, which is of the law, but you must have the righteousness of Christ. Therefore, come unto the Lord Jesus Christ, and He will give it to you; He will not send you away without it. Receive Him upon His own terms, and He is yours forever: O devote yourselves to Him, soul and body, and all, to be His forever; and Christ will be yours and then happy, happy you, that ever you were born!

("Christ, the Best Husband")

Arrogant Intellectuals

Men of low and narrow minds soon commence wise in their own conceits: and having acquired a little smattering of the learned languages, and made some small proficiency in the dry sciences, are easily tempted to look upon themselves as a head taller than their fellow mortals, and accordingly too, too often put forth great swelling words of vanity. But persons of a more exalted, and extensive reach of thought, dare not boast. No, they know that the greatest scholars are in the dark in respect to many even of the minutest things in life. And after all their painful researches into the Arcana Natura, they find such an immense void, such an immeasurable expanse yet to be traveled over, that they are obliged at last to conclude, almost with respect to every thing, "that they know nothing yet as they ought to know." This consideration, no doubt, led Socrates, when he was asked by one of his scholars, why the oracle pronounced him the wisest man on earth, to give him this judicious answer, "Perhaps it is, because I am most sensible of my own ignorance." Would to God, that all who call themselves Christians had learned so much as this heathen! We should then no longer hear so many learned men, falsely so called, betray their ignorance by boasting of the extent of their shallow understanding, nor by professing themselves so wise, prove themselves such arrant pedantic fools.

("The Potter and the Clay")

Darkened Understanding

I f we view our understandings in respect to spiritual things, we shall find that they are not only darkened, but become darkness itself, even "darkness that may be felt" by all who are not past feeling. And how should it be otherwise, since the infallible word of God assures us, that they are alienated from the light of life of God, and thereby naturally as incapable to judge of divine and spiritual things, comparatively speaking, as a man born blind is incapacitated to distinguish the various colors of the rainbow.

("The Potter and the Clay")

Preparation for Heaven

I suppose, I may take it for granted, that all of you amongst whom I am now preaching the kingdom of God, hope after death to go to a place which we call Heaven. And my heart's desire and prayer to God for you is, that you all may have mansions prepared for you there. But give me leave to tell you, were you now to see these heavens opened, and the angel (to use the words of the seraphic Hervey clothed with all his heavenly drapery, with one foot upon the earth, and another upon the sea; nay, were you to see and hear the angel of the everlasting covenant, Jesus Christ Himself, proclaiming "time shall be no more," and giving you all an invitation immediately to come to Heaven. Heaven would be no heaven to you; nay it would be a Hell to your souls, unless you were first prepared for a proper enjoyment of it here on earth. "For what communion hath light with darkness?" Or what fellowship could unrenewed sons of Belial possibly keep up with the pure and immaculate Jesus?

("The Potter and the Clay")

Repentance

This moral change is what some call, repentance; some, conversion; some, regeneration. Choose what name you please, I only pray God, that we all may have the thing. The scriptures call it holiness, sanctification, the new creature. Our Lord calls it a "New birth, or being born again, or born from above." These are not merely figurative expressions, or the flights of Eastern language, nor do they barely denote a relative change of state conferred on all those who are admitted into Christ's church by baptism. But they denote a real, moral change of heart and life, a real participation of the divine life in the soul of man. Some indeed content themselves with a figurative interpretation; but unless they are made to experience the power and efficacy thereof, by a solid living experience in their own souls, all their learning, all their labored criticism, will not exempt them from a real damnation. Christ has said it, and Christ will stand, "Unless a man," learned or unlearned, high or low, though he be a master of Israel as Nicodemus was, unless he "be born again, he cannot see, he cannot enter into the kingdom of God."

("The Potter and the Clay")

Reasoning with Sinners

And I am so far from thinking that Christian preachers should not make use of rational arguments and motives in their sermons, that I cannot think they are fit to preach at all, who either cannot or will not use them. We have the example of the great God himself for such a practice: "Come (says He) and let us reason together." And St. Paul, that prince of preachers, "reasoned of temperance, and righteousness, and a judgment to come." And it is remarkable, "that whilst he was reasoning of these things, Felix trembled." Nor are the most persuasive strains of holy rhetoric less needful for a scribe ready instructed to the kingdom of God. The scriptures both of the Old and New Testament everywhere abound with them. And when can they be more properly employed, and brought forth, than when we are acting as ambassadors of Heaven, and beseeching poor sinners, as in Christ's stead, to be reconciled unto God.

("The Potter and the Clay")

Ingratitude

Numberless marks does man bear in his soul, that he is fallen and estranged from God; but nothing gives a greater proof thereof, than that backwardness, which everyone finds within himself, to the duty of praise and thanksgiving.

("Thankfulness for Mercies Received, A Necessary Duty")

Lessons From Sailors

When I have seen you preparing for a storm, and reefing your sails to guard against it; how have I wished that you and I were as careful to avoid that storm of God's wrath, which will certainly, without repentance, quickly overtake us. When I have observed you catch at ever fair gale, how I secretly cried, O that we were as careful to know the things that belong to our peace, before they are forever hidden from our eyes! And when I have taken notice, how steadily you eyed your compass in order to steer aright, how have I wished, that we as steadily eyed the word of God, which alone can preserve us from "making shipwreck of faith, and a good conscience!" In short, there is scarce anything you do, which has not been a lesson of instruction to me; and, therefore, it would be ungrateful in me, did I not take this opportunity of exhorting you in the name of our Lord Jesus Christ, to be as wise in the things which concern you soul, as I have observed you to be in the affairs belonging to your ship.

("Thankfulness for Mercies Received")

Self Righteousness

But, however contrary to the doctrines of the Church of England, yet our pulpits ring of nothing more, than doing no one any harm, living honestly, loving your neighbor as yourselves, and do what you can, and then Christ is to make up the deficiency. This is making Christ to be half a savior, and man the other part; but I say, Christ will be your whole righteousness, your whole wisdom, your whole sanctification, or else He will never be your whole redemption.

("Christ, the Support of the Tempted")

Sinful Nature

But let these modern, polite gentlemen, and let my letter-learned brethren, paint man in as lovely colors as they please, I will not do it; I dare not make him better than the Word of God does. If I was to paint man in his proper colors, I must go to the kingdom of Hell for a copy; for man is by nature full of pride, subtlety, malice, envy, revenge, and all uncharitableness; and what are these but the temper of the devil? And lust, sensuality, pleasure, these are the tempers of the beast. Thus, my brethren, man is half a beast, and half a devil, a motley mixture of the beast and devil.

("Christ, the Support of the Tempted")

False Converts at Church

O my brethren, do not give the devil a handle wherewith he may lay hold on you. Alas! it is not wonder that the devil tempts you, when he finds you at a play, a ball, or masquerade; if you are doing the devil's work, it is no wonder if he presses you in the continuation thereof; and how can any say, "Lead us not into temptation," in the morning, when they are resolved to run into it at night? Good God! Are these persons members of the Church of England? Alas, when you have gone to church, and read over the prayers, it is offering no more than the sacrifice of fools; you say Amen to them with your lips, when in your hearts you are either unconcerned at what you are about, or else you think that the bare saying of your prayers is sufficient, and that then God and you have balanced accounts.

("Christ, the Support of the Tempted")

Failure of Hecklers

And very often, when the people of God are met to worship him, he sends his agents, the scoffers, to disturb them. We saw an instance of their rage just now; they would fain have disturb us; but the Lord was on our side, and so prevented all the attempts of wicked and designing men, to disturb and disquiet us. Lord Jesus, forgive them who are thus persecuting your truth! Jesus, show them that they are fighting against you, and that it is hard for them to kick against the pricks!

("Christ, the Support of the Tempted")

When open air preaching, you may have a few concerns. Perhaps one of them is the thought of someone verbally disagreeing with what you say. These folk are what are known as "hecklers."

While it seems that Whitefield had a disrupting heckler on this occasion, the best thing that can happen to an open air meeting is to have a good heckler. Jesus gave us some of the greatest gems of Scripture because someone either made a statement or asked a question in an open air setting. A good heckler can increase a crowd of 20 people to 200 in a matter of minutes. The air becomes electric. Suddenly, you have 200 people listening intently to how you will answer a heckler.

All you have to do is remember the attributes of 2 Timothy 2:23-26: Be patient, gentle, humble. Don't worry if you can't answer a question. Just say, "I can't answer that, but I'll try to get the answer for you if you really want to know." With Bible "difficulties," I regularly fall back on the powerful statement of Mark Twain: "Most people are bothered by those passages of Scripture they don't understand, but for me, I have always noticed that the passages that bother me are those I do understand."

A "good" heckler is one who will provoke your thoughts. He will stand up, speak up, and then shut up so that you can preach. Occasionally, you will get hecklers who have the first two qualifications, but they just won't be quiet. If they will not let you get a word in, move your location. Most of the crowd will follow. Better to have ten listeners who can hear than 200 who can't. If the heckler follows, move again ... then the crowd will usually turn on him.

One ploy that often works with a heckler, who is out solely to hinder the Gospel, is to wait until he is quiet and say to the crowd (making sure the heckler is listening also), "I want to show you how people are like sheep. When I move, watch this man follow me because he can't get a crowd by himself." His pride usually keeps him from following.

If you have a "mumbling heckler" who won't speak up, ignore him and talk over the top of him. This will usually get him angry enough to speak up and draw hearers. There is a fine line between him getting angry enough to draw a crowd ... and hitting you; you will find it in time.

If you are fortunate enough to get a heckler, don't panic. Show him genuine respect, not only because he can double your crowd, but because the Bible says to honor all men, so you don't want to offend him unnecessarily. Ask the heckler his name, so that if you want to ask him a question and he is talking to someone, you don't have to say, "Hey you!"

Often, people will walk through the crowd so they can get close to you and will whisper something like, "I think you are a #@*!$!" Answer loud enough for the crowd to hear, "God bless you." Do it with a smile so that it looks as though the person has just whispered a word of encouragement to you. This will stop him from doing it again. The Bible says to bless those who curse you, and to do good to those who hate you. Remember that you are not fighting against flesh and blood.

Hecklers will stoop very low and be cutting and cruel in their remarks. If you have some physical disability, they will play on it. Try to smile back at them. Look past the words. If you are reviled for the name of Jesus, "rejoice, and be exceeding glad." Read Matthew 5:10-12 until it is written on the corridors of your mind.

The most angry hecklers are usually what we call "backsliders." These are actually false converts who never *slid forward in the first place. They "asked Jesus into their heart," but never truly repented. Ask him, "Did you know the Lord?" (See Hebrews 8:11.) If he answers, "Yes," then he is admitting that he is willfully denying Him. If he answers, "No," then he was never a Christian in the first place—"This is eternal life, that they might know you, the only true God, and Jesus Christ, whom you have sent" (John 17:3). — Ray Comfort*

Not Ashamed

T he devil and his agents have their clubs of reveling, and their societies of drunkenness. They are not ashamed to be seen and heard doing the devil their master's works; they are not ashamed to proclaim him; and sure you are not ashamed of the Lord Jesus Christ. You dare proclaim that Jesus, who died that you might live, and who will own you before His Father and all the holy angels. Therefore, dare to be singularly good. Be not afraid of the face of man; let not all the threats of the men of this world move you. What is the loss of all the grandeur, or pleasure, or reputation of this life, compared to the loss of Heaven, of Christ and of your souls? And as for the reproaches of the world, do not mind them; when they revile you, never, never revile again; do not answer railing with railing; but let love, kindness, meekness, patience, long-suffering, be found in you, as they were in the blessed Jesus. Therefore, I beseech you, do not neglect the frequent coming together, and telling each other, what great things Jesus Christ hath done for your souls.

("Christ, the Support of the Tempted")

Salvation Offered to Hecklers

O you scoffers, come and see this Jesus, this Lord of glory whom you have despised; and if you will but come to Christ, He will be willing to receive you, notwithstanding all the persecution you have used towards His members. However, if you are resolved to persist in your obstinacy, remember, salvation was offered to you, that Christ and free grace were proposed; but you refused to accept of either, and therefore your blood will be required at your own hands.

("Christ, the Support of the Tempted")

Slandered for the Gospel's Sake

B ut he is unworthy the name of a minister of the gospel of peace, who is unwilling, not only to have his name cast out as evil, but also to die for the truths of the Lord Jesus. It is the character of hirelings and false prophets, who care not for the sheep, to have all men speak well of them.

("What Think You of Christ?")

God Gives Grace to the Humble

W e must not come to God as the proud Pharisee did, bringing in as it were a reckoning of our services. We must come in the temper and language of the poor Publican, smiting upon our breasts, and saying, "God be merciful to me a sinner;" for Jesus Christ justifies us while we are ungodly. He came not to call the righteous, but sinners to repentance. The poor in spirit, only they who are willing to go out of themselves, and rely wholly on the righteousness of another, are so blessed as to be members of His kingdom.

("What Think You of Christ?")

As you share the Gospel, divorce yourself from the thought that you are merely seeking "decisions for Christ." What we should be seeking is repentance within the heart. This is the purpose of the Law, to bring the knowledge of sin. How can a man repent if he doesn't know what sin is? If there is no repentance, there is no salvation. Jesus said, "Unless you repent, you shall all likewise perish" (Luke 13:3). God is not willing that any should perish, but that all should come to repentance (2 Peter 3:9).

Many don't understand that the salvation of a soul is not a resolution to change a way of life, but "repentance toward God, and faith toward our Lord Jesus Christ."

The modern concept of success in evangelism is to relate how many people were "saved" (that is, how many prayed the "sinner's prayer"). This produces a "no decisions, no success" mentality. This shouldn't be, because Christians who seek decisions in evangelism become discouraged after a time of witnessing if "no one came to the Lord."

The Bible tells us that as we sow the good seed of the Gospel, one sows and another reaps. If you faithfully sow the seed, someone will reap. If you reap, it is because someone has sown in the past, but it is God who causes the seed to grow. If His hand is not on the person you are leading in a prayer of committal, if there is not God-given repentance, then you will end up with a stillbirth on your hands, and that is nothing to rejoice about.

We should measure our success by how faithfully we sowed the seed. In that way, we will avoid becoming discouraged. Billy Graham said, "If you have not repented, you will not see the inside of the Kingdom of God." — Ray Comfort

Assurance of Salvation

F or Christ came to save us not only from the guilt, but also from the power of our sins. Till He has done this, however, He may be a Savior to others, we can have no assurance of well-grounded hope, that He has saved us. For it is by receiving His blessed Spirit into our hearts, and feeling Him witnessing with our spirits, that we are the sons of God, that we can be certified of our being sealed to the day of redemption.

("What Think You of Christ?")

Consider Your Soul

H owever lightly you may esteem your souls, I know our Lord has set an unspeakable value on them. He thought them worthy of His most precious blood. I beseech you, therefore, O sinners, be ye reconciled to God.

("What Think You of Christ?")

Possibility of Death

Though this is Saturday night, and you are now preparing for the Sabbath, for what you know, you may yet never live to see the Sabbath. You have had awful proofs of this lately; a woman died but yesterday, a man died the day before, another was killed by something that fell from a house, and it may be in twenty-four hours more, many of you may be carried into an unalterable state. Now then, for God's sake, for your own souls sake, if ye have a mind to dwell with God, and cannot bear the thought of dwelling in everlasting burning, before I go any further, silently put up one prayer, or say Amen to the prayer I would put in your mouths; "Lord, search me and try me, Lord, examine my heart, and let my conscience speak; O let me know whether I am converted or not!" What say you, my dear hearers? What say you, my fellow-sinners? What say you, my guilty brethren? Has God by His blessed Spirit wrought such a change in your hearts?

("Marks of a True Conversion")

It is a great benefit in preaching to appeal to the will to live in sinners. God has placed eternity in the hearts of all of us. Every sane person has a cry, "Oh, I don't want to die!" Appeal to that God-given will to live. — *Ray Comfort*

Fruits of Salvation

If God be your father, obey Him: if God be your father, serve Him. Love Him with all your heart, love Him with all your might, with all your soul, and with all your strength. If God is your father, fly from everything that may displease Him; and walk worthy of that God, who has called you to His kingdom and glory. If you are converted and become like little children, then behave as little children: they long for the breast, and with it will be contented. Are you newborn babes? Then desire the sincere milk of the word that you may grow thereby.

("Marks of a True Conversion")

Self Examination

E xamine yourselves, therefore, my brethren, whether you are in the faith; prove yourselves; and think it not sufficient to say in your creed, I believe in Jesus Christ; many say so, who do not believe, who are reprobates, and yet in a state of death. You take God's name in vain, when you call him Father, and your prayers are turned into sin, unless you believe in Christ, so as to have your life hid with Him in God, and to receive life and nourishment from Him, as branches do from the vine.

("What Think You of Christ?")

Sinner's Prayer

A nd therefore, as I suppose many of you are unconverted, and graceless, go home! Away to your closets, and down with your stubborn hearts before God. If you have not done it before, let this be the night. Or, do not stay till you go home; begin now while standing here; pray to God, and let the language of your heart be, Lord, convert me! Lord, make me a little child. Lord Jesus, let me not be banished from your kingdom!

("Marks of a True Conversion")

Tears in His Voice

O that my head were waters, O that mine eyes were a fountain of tears, that I might weep over an unconverted, graceless, wicked, and adulterous generation. Precious souls, for God's sake, think what will become of you when you die, if you die without being converted. If you go hence without the wedding garment, God will strike you speechless, and you shall be banished from His presence forever and ever. I know you cannot dwell with everlasting burnings; behold then I show you a way of escape. Jesus is the way, Jesus is the truth, the Lord Jesus Christ is the resurrection and the life.

("Marks of a True Conversion")

Being Good Enough

You may say over your prayers all your lives, and yet you may never pray over one: therefore, while you flatter yourselves you are good enough, and that you are in a state of salvation, you are only deceiving you own souls, and hastening on your own destruction. Come unto Him, not as being good enough, but as vile sinners, as poor, and blind, and naked, and miserable, and then Jesus will have compassion.

("Christ, the Only Rest...")

Hypocrisy

You Pharisees, who are going about to establish your own righteousness; you, who are too polite to follow the Lord Jesus Christ in sincerity and truth; you, who are all for a little show, a little outside work; who lead moral, civil, decent lives, Christ will not know you at the great day, but will say unto you, O ye Pharisees, was there any place for me in your love? Alas! you are full of anger and malice, and self-will; yet you pretended to love and serve me, and to be my people: but, however, I despise you; I, who am God, and knows the secret of all hearts; I, who am truth itself, the faithful and true witness, say unto you, "Depart from me, you workers of iniquity, into that place of torment, prepared for the devil and his angels."

("Christ, the Only Rest...")

The Danger for Law Breakers

And must these discreet polite creatures, who never did anyone harm, but led such civil, decent lives, must they suffer the vengeance of eternal fire? Cannot their righteous souls be saved? Where then must the sinner and the ungodly appear? Where will you, O Sabbath-breaker, appear, you, who can take your pleasure, your recreation, on the Lord's-day, who refuses to hear the word of God, who will not come to church to be instructed in the ways of the Lord? Where will you, O you adulterers, fornicators, and such-like of this generation appear? Whoremongers and adulterers, God will judge, and them He will condemn. Then you will not call these tricks of youth: no, but you will call on the rocks and the mountains to fall on you, to hide you from the fury and anger of the Lord.

("Christ, the Only Rest")

The Work of the Law

You, who are awakened to a sense of your sins, who see how hateful they are to God, and how they lay you open to His wrath and indignation, and would willingly avoid them; who hate yourselves for committing them; when you are thus convinced of sin, when you see the terrors of the Law, and are afraid of His judgments; then you may be said to be weary of your sins. And O how terrible do they appear when you are first awakened to a sense of them; when you see nothing but the wrath of God ready to fall upon you, and you are afraid of His judgments! O how heavy is your sin to you then! Then you feel the weight thereof, and that it is grievous to be born.

("Christ, the Only Rest")

Repentance and Faith

It is not, my brethren, coming with your own works: no, you must come in full dependence upon the Lord Jesus Christ, looking on Him as the Lord who died to save sinners.

Go to Him, tell Him you are lost, undone, miserable sinners and that you deserve nothing but Hell. When you thus go to the Lord Jesus Christ out of yourself, in full dependence on the Lord Jesus Christ, you will find Him an able and a willing savior. He is pleased to see sinners coming to Him in a sense of their own unworthiness; and when their case seems to be most dangerous, most distressed, then the Lord in His mercy steps in and gives you His grace. He puts His Spirit within you, takes away your heart of stone, and gives you a heart of flesh. Stand not out then against this Lord, but go unto Him, not in your own strength, but in the strength of Jesus Christ.

("Christ, the Only Rest")

Law-Breakers Invited

Come then by faith, and lay hold of the Lord Jesus; though he is in Heaven, He now calls you. Come, all you drunkards, swearers, Sabbath-breakers, adulterers, fornicators; come, all you scoffers, harlots, thieves, and murderers, and Jesus Christ will save you. He will give you rest, if you are weary of your sins. O come lay hold upon Him. Had I less love for your souls, I might speak less; but that love of God, which is shed abroad in my heart, will not permit me to leave you, till I see whether you will come to Christ or not.

("Christ, the Only Rest")

Judgment Day

The promiscuous dispensations of providence in this life, wherein we see good men afflicted, destitute, tormented, and the wicked permitted triumphantly to ride over their heads, has been always looked upon as an indisputable argument, by the generality of men, that there will be a day in which God will judge the world in righteousness, and administer equity unto His people. Some indeed are so bold as to deny it, while they are engaged in the pursuit of the lust of the eye, and the pride of life. But follow them to their death bed, ask them, when their souls are ready to launch into eternity, what they then think of a judgment to come and they will tell you, they dare not give their consciences the lie any longer. They feel a fearful looking for of judgment and fiery indignation in their hearts. Since then these things are so, does it not highly concern each of us, my brethren, before we come on a bed of sickness, seriously to examine how the account stands between God and our souls, and how it will fare with us in that day?

As for the openly profane, the drunkard, the whoremonger, the adulterer, and such-like, there is no doubt of what will become of them. Without repentance they shall never enter into the kingdom of God and His Christ. No; their damnation slumbers not; a burning fiery Tophet, kindled by the fury of God's eternal wrath, is prepared for their reception, wherein they must suffer the vengeance of eternal fire. Nor is there the least doubt of the state of true believers. For though they are despised and rejected of natural men, yet being born again of God, they are heirs of God, and joint heirs with Christ. They have the earnest of the promised inheritance in their hearts, and are assured that a new and living way is made open for them, into the holy of holies, by the blood of Jesus

Christ, into which an abundant entrance shall be administered to them at the great day of account.

("The Wise and Foolish Virgins")

The Lawless Without Hope

And if persons may go to church, receive the sacrament, lead honest moral lives, and yet be sent to Hell at the last day, as they certainly will be if they advance no farther, Where will you, O drunkard? Where will you, O swearer? Where will you, O Sabbath-breaker? Where will you that deny divine revelation, and even the form of godliness? Where will you, and such like sinners appear?

("The Wise and Foolish Virgins")

Whitefield's Determination to Preach

If they will not let me preach Christ crucified, and offer salvation to poor sinners in a church, I will preach him in the lanes, streets, highways and hedges; and nothing pleases me better, than to think I am now in one of the devil's strongest holds.

("The Wise and Foolish Virgins")

The Almost Christian in Hell

O foolish mortal that I was, thus to bring myself into these never-ceasing tortures, for the transitory enjoyment of a few short-lived pleasures, which scarcely afforded me any satisfaction, even when I most indulged myself in them. Alas! Are these the wages, these the effects of sin? O damned apostate! First to delude me with pretended promises of happiness, and after several years drudgery in his service, thus to involve me in eternal woe. O that I had never hearkened to his beguiling insinuations! O that I had rejected his very first suggestions with the utmost detestation and abhorrence! O that I had taken up my cross and followed Christ! O that I had never ridiculed serious godliness; and out of a false politeness, condemned the truly pious as too severe, enthusiastic, or superstitious! For I then had been happy indeed, happy beyond expression, happy to all eternity, yonder in those blessed regions where they fit, clothed with unspeakable glory, and chanting forth their seraphic hallelujahs to the Lamb that sits upon the throne forever. But, alas! These reflections come now too late; these wishes now are vain and fruitless. I have not suffered, and therefore must not reign with them. I have in effect denied the Lord that bought me, and therefore, justly am I now denied by Him. But must I live forever tormented in these flames? Must this body of mine, which not long since lay in state, was clothed in purple and fine linen, and fared sumptuously every day, must it be here eternally confined, and made the mockery of insulting devils? O eternity! That thought fills me with despair: I must be miserable forever.

("The Eternity of Hell's Torments")

Lukewarm Christians Warned

Come, all you Christians of a lukewarm, Laodicean spirit, you Gallies in religion, who care a little, but not enough for the things of God. O think, think with yourselves, how deplorable it will be to lose the enjoyment of Heaven, and run into endless torments, merely because you will be content to be almost, and will not strive to be altogether Christians. Consider, I beseech you to consider, how you will rave and curse that fatal stupidity which made you believe anything less than true faith in Jesus, productive of a life of strict piety, self-denial, and mortification, can keep you from those torments, the eternity of which I have been endeavoring to prove.

("The Eternity of Hell's Torments")

He Is a Good Master

Consider, if you do not, your damnation is from yourselves. Must I weep over you as our Savior did over Jerusalem? I beseech you, by all that is good and dear to you, do not cast away your souls forever. O mind, in this your day, the things that belong to your peace, before they are forever hidden from your eyes. Could I speak with the tongues of men or angels, with all the rhetoric possible, I could never tell the worth of Christ. He is a good Master; indeed He is. I wish all that hear me this day would lay hold on Him, by faith, and take Him on His own terms. Do not be angry with me for my love. How glad would I be to bring some of you to God! Come! He calls you by His ministers. Bring your sins with you, that He may make you saints. He will sanctify all who believe on Him."

("Watching, the Peculiar Duty of a Christian" from Tyerman, Vol. 1, p. 304.)

The Knowledge of Christ

The Lord Jesus Christ takes notice of each of you, you may think the Lord does not take notice of us, because we are in a field, and out of church walls; but He does observe with what view you came this evening to hear His word. He knows whether it was to satisfy your curiosity, or to find out wherewith you might ridicule the preacher. The thoughts and intentions of all your hearts are not hidden from Jesus Christ. Though He may seem to be asleep, because you are, at present, insensible of His workings upon your heart, and He may not seem to take notice of you, and regard you, no more than He did the Syrophoenician woman. Yet He will turn to you and behold you with love; the Lord will be mindful of you in due time, and speak peace to your troubled soul, though the sea of troubles is beating over you, though the Pharisees of this day are scoffing at you, yet, when Christ rebukes, then they shall cease.

("The Folly and Danger of Parting with Christ...")

Sins Do Not Hinder Salvation

And so, my brethren, I may say to you, why are you fearful to leave you sins and turn to God? O turn to Him, turn in a sense of your own unworthiness; tell Him how polluted you are, how vile, and be not faithless, but believe. Do not go in your own strength, and then you need not fear. Why fear that the Lord Jesus Christ will not accept you? Your sins will be no hindrance, your unworthiness will be no hindrance; if your own corrupt hearts do not keep you back, or if your own good works do not hinder you from coming, nothing will hinder Christ from receiving of you. He loves to see poor sinners coming to Him, He is pleased to see them lie at His feet pleading His promises: and if you thus come to Christ, He will not send you away without His Spirit; no, but will receive and bless you.

("The Folly and Danger of Parting with Christ...")

Ease in the Storm of Sin

If you are easy under the storm and tempest of sin, and do not cry to Christ for salvation, you are in a dangerous condition. And it is a wonder to consider, how a man that is not sure of having made his peace with God, can eat, or drink, or live in peace; that you are not afraid, when you lie down, that you should awake in Hell. But if Christ speaks peace to your soul, who can then speak trouble? None; no, not men or devils. Therefore, lie down at the feet of Christ whom you have resisted, and say, Lord, what would you have me to do? And He will rebuke the winds and seas of your troubled mind, and all things will be calm.

("The Folly and Danger of Parting with Christ...")

God Resists the Proud

Do not flatter yourselves of being good enough, because you are morally so; because you go to church, say the prayers, and take the sacrament, therefore you think no more is required. Alas, you are deceiving your own souls; and if God, in His free grace and mercy, does not show you your error, it will only be leading you a softer way to your eternal ruin. But God forbid that any of you, to whom I am now speaking, should imagine this; no, you must be abased, and God must be exalted, or you will never begin at the right end. You will never see Jesus with comfort or satisfaction, unless you go to Him only on the account of what He has done and suffered.

("The Folly and Danger of Parting with Christ...")

<hr/>

Preachers as Witnesses at Judgment Day

How will you be able to stand at the bar of an angry, sin-avenging judge, and see so many discourses you have despised, so many ministers, who once longed and labored for the salvation of your precious and immortal souls, brought out as so many swift witnesses against you? Will it be sufficient then, think you, to allege, that you went to hear them only out of curiosity, to pass away an idle hour, to admire the oratory, or ridicule the simplicity of the preacher? No; God will then let you know, that you ought to have come out of better principles; that every sermon has been put down to your account, and that you must then be justly punished for not improving by them.

("Directions How to Hear Sermons")

The Nearness of Judgment

ₛee that emblem of human life," said he as he pointed at a flitting shadow. "It passed for a moment, and concealed the brightness of Heaven from our view; but it is gone. And where will you be, my hearers, when your lives have passed away like that dark cloud? Oh, my dear friends, I see thousands sitting attentive, with their eyes fixed on the poor unworthy preacher. In a few days, we shall all meet at the judgment seat of Christ. We shall form a part of that vast assembly which will gather before His throne. Every eye will behold the Judge. With a voice whose call you must abide and answer, He will inquire, whether on earth you strove to enter in at the strait gate; whether you were supremely devoted to God; whether your hearts were absorbed in Him. My blood runs cold when I think how many of you will then seek to enter in, and shall not be able. O, what plea can you make before the Judge of the whole earth?"

(Tyerman, Vol. 1, pp. 419-20.)

Prayer

O prayer," cried the impassioned preacher, in another part of his conference sermon, "O prayer, prayer! It brings and keeps God and man together; it raises man up to God, and brings God down to man. If you would keep up your walk with God, pray, pray without ceasing. Be much in secret, set prayer. When you are about the common business of life, be much in ejaculatory prayer. Send, from time to time, short letter posts to Heaven, upon the wings of faith. They will reach the very heart of God, and will return to you loaded with blessings."

(Tyerman, Vol. 2, p. 56.)

A New Heart

I tell you, O man; I tell you O woman, whoever you are, you are a dead man, you are a dead woman, no a damned man, a damned woman, without a new heart.

(From "The Putting on of the New Man, A Certain Mark of the Real Christian," quoted in Tyerman, Vol. 2, p. 242.)

You Cannot Do Without the Grace of God

Are any of you here unconverted? No doubt too many. Are any of you come this morning, out of curiosity, to hear what the babbler has to say? Many, perhaps, are glad it is my last sermon, and that London is to be rid of such a monster; but surely you cannot be angry with me for my wishing that the grace of God may be with you all. O that it may be with every unconverted soul! O man! What will you do if the grace of God is not with you? My brethren, you cannot do without the grace of God when you come to die. Do you know that without this you are nothing but devils incarnate? Do you know that every moment you are liable to eternal pains? Don't say I part with you in an ill humor. Don't say that a madman left you with a curse. Blessed be God! When I first became a field preacher, I proclaimed the grace of God to the worst of sinners; and I proclaim it now to the vilest sinner under Heaven. Could I speak so loud that the whole world might hear me, I would declare that the grace of God is free for all who are willing to accept of it by Christ. God make you all willing this day!

(From a sermon preached on Feb. 23, 1763, quoted in Tyerman, Vol. 2, pp. 459-60.)

The Torments of Hell

Make God your refuge. If you stop short of this, you will only be a sport for devils. There is no river to make glad the inhabitants of hell: no streams to cool them in that scorching element. Were those in Hell to have such an offer of mercy as you have, how would their chains rattle! How would they come with the flames of Hell about their ears! Fly! Sinner fly! God help you to fly to Himself for refuge! Hark! Hear the Word of the Lord! See the world consumed! See the avenger of blood at your heels! If you do not take refuge in God tonight, you may tomorrow be damned forever!

(Tyerman, Vol. 2, p. 460.)

Weeping Over Sinners

Don't be angry with a poor minister for weeping over them who will not weep for themselves. If you laugh at me, I know Jesus smiles. I am free from the blood of you all. If you are damned for want of conversion, remember you are not damned for want of warning.

(Tyerman, Vol. 2, p. 460.)

Self Examination

In your Bibles, you have registered your births; and some of you the time when you were born again; but are you new creatures now?

(Tyerman, Vol. 2, p. 462.)

All the World Is My Parish

I profess to be a member of the Church of England; but if they will not let me preach in a church, I will preach anywhere. All the world is my parish; and I will preach wherever God gives me opportunity. You will never find me disputing about the outward appendages of religion. Don't tell me you are a Baptist, an Independent, a Presbyterian, a Dissenter: tell me you are a Christian. That is all I want. This is the religion of Heaven and must be ours upon earth.

(Tyerman, Vol. 2, p. 567.)

The Terrors of the Lord

When I saw you from my study crowding to come in, when I saw you pushing forward, some to go up to the tabernacle, or into the vestry, some to fill the area, and others to stand at the door, I thought, "How shall I manage with myself tonight? Shall I endeavor to make these weep and cry? Shall I not earnestly address so many precious souls in a practical way, to bring them not to the preacher, but to the preacher's master? Knowing the terrors of the Lord, we would fain persuade all to flee from the wrath to come.

(*20 Centuries of Great Preaching; Volume 3*, Waco, TX: Word Books Publishing, 1974, p. 114.)

I love those that thunder out the Word. The Christian world is in a deep sleep! Nothing but a loud voice can awaken them out of it.

(*George Whitefield; God's Anointed Servant in the Great Revival of the Eighteenth Century*, by Arnold A. Dallimore, Wheaton, IL: Crossway Books, 1990, p. 67.)

O that I could do more for Him! O that I was a flame of pure and holy fire, and had a thousand lives to spend in the dear Redeemer's Service ... The sight of so many perishing souls affects me much, and makes me long to go if possible from pole to pole, to proclaim redeeming love.

(*George Whitefield; God's Anointed Servant in the Great Revival of the Eighteenth Century*, by Arnold A. Dallimore, Wheaton, IL: Crossway Books, 1990, p. 149.)

What a pity it is that modern preachers attend no more to the method those took who were first inspired by the Holy Ghost, in preaching Jesus Christ! The success they were honored with, gave a sanction to their manner of preaching, and the divine authority of their discourses, and energy of their elocution, one would think, should have more weight with those that are called to dispense the gospel, than all modern schemes whatever. If this was the case, ministers would then learn first to sow, and then to reap; they would endeavor to plough up the fallow ground, and thereby prepare the people for God's raining down blessing upon them.

(20 Centuries of Great Preaching; Volume 3, Waco, TX: Word Books Publishing, 1974, p. 137.)

———•••———

It is clear from Scripture that God requires us to not only preach to sinners, but also to teach them. The servant of the Lord must be "able to teach, patient, in meekness instructing" those who oppose them (2 Timothy 2:24-25).

For a long while, I thought I was to leap among sinners, scatter the seed, then leave. But our responsibility goes further. We are to bring the sinner to a point of understanding his need before God. Psalm 25:8 says, "Good and upright is the LORD: therefore will he teach sinners in the way."

Psalm 51:13 adds, "Then will I teach transgressors your ways; and sinners shall be converted to you."

The Great Commission is to teach sinners: "Teach all nations ... teaching them to observe all things" (Matthew 28:19-20). The disciples obeyed the command "daily in the temple, and in every house, they ceased not to teach and preach Jesus Christ" (Acts 5:42, emphasis added). The "good-soil" hearer is he who "hears ... and understands" (Matthew 13:23).

Philip, the evangelist, saw fit to ask his potential convert, the Ethiopian, "Do you understand what you are reading?" Some preachers are like a loud gun that misses the target. It may sound effective, but if the bullet misses the target, the exercise is in vain. He may be the largest-lunged, chandelier-swinging, pulpit-pounding preacher this side of the Book of Acts. *He may have great teaching on faith, and everyone he touches may fall over, but if the sinner leaves the meeting failing to understand his desperate need of God's forgiveness, then the preacher has failed. He has missed the target, which is the understanding of the sinner. This is why the Law of God must be used in preaching. It is a "schoolmaster" to bring "the knowledge of sin." It teaches and instructs. A sinner will come to "know His will, and approve the things that are more excellent," if he is "instructed out of the Law" (Romans 2:18).* — Ray Comfort

Pleading with the Young Men and Women

B ut I must speak a word to you, young maidens, as well as young men. I see many of you adorned as to your bodies, but are your souls naked? Which of you can say, "The Lord is my righteousness"? Which of you ever desired to be dressed in this robe of invaluable price, without which you are no better than whited sepulchers in the sight of God? (See Matthew 23:27.) Young maidens do not forget any longer your chief and only ornament. Oh, seek for the Lord to be your righteousness, or otherwise burning will soon be upon you instead of beauty!

(*The World's Greatest Preachers*, compiled by Ray Comfort and Kirk Cameron, New Kensington, PA: Whitaker House, 2003, p. 83.)

Pleading with the Middle-aged

A nd what will I say to those of you of middle-age, you busy merchants, you cumbered Martha's, who, with all your gains, have not yet gotten the Lord to be your righteousness? Alas, what profit will there be of all your labor under the sun if you do not secure this pearl of invaluable price? (See Matthew 13:46.) This one thing, so absolutely needful, that it alone can stand in your place when all other things are taken from you. Therefore, do not anxiously labor any longer for the meat that perishes, but from now on seek the Lord to be your righteousness, a righteousness that will entitle you to life everlasting.

(The World's Greatest Preachers, compiled by Ray Comfort and Kirk Cameron, New Kensington, PA: Whitaker House, 2003, p. 83.)

Pleading with the Elderly

I see also many hoary heads here, and perhaps the most of them cannot say, "The Lord is my righteousness." O gray-headed sinner, I could weep over you! Your gray hairs, which ought to be your crown, and in which perhaps you glory, are now your shame. You do not know that the Lord is your righteousness. Oh, haste then, haste, aged sinners, and seek redeeming love! Alas, you have one foot already in the grave, your glass is just run out, your sun is just going down, and it will set and leave you in an eternal darkness unless the Lord is your righteousness! Flee then, oh flee for your lives! Do not be afraid. All things are possible with God. If you come, though it be at the eleventh hour, Christ Jesus will by no means cast you out. Seek then for the Lord to be your righteousness, and beseech Him to let you know how it is that a man may be born again when he is old!

(*The World's Greatest Preachers,* compiled by Ray Comfort and Kirk Cameron, New Kensington, PA: Whitaker House, 2003, pp. 83-84.)

———•·•———

You must be converted, or be damned, and that is plain English, but not plainer than my Master made us of, "He that believeth not, shall be damned." I did not speak that word strong enough that says, "He that believeth not shall be damned;" that is the language of our Lord; and it is said of one of the primitive preachers, that used to speak the word damned so that it struck all his auditory. We are afraid of speaking the word damned for fear of offending such and such a one; at the same time they despise the minister for not being honest to his master.

20 Centuries of Great Preaching; Volume 3 (Waco, TX: Word Books Publishing, 1974), p. 143.

If you are damned for want of conversion, remember you are not damned for want of warning. Thousands that have not the gospel preached to them, may say, Lord, we never heard what conversion is; but you are gospel-proof; and if there is any deeper place in Hell than another, God will order a gospel-despising Methodist to be put there. You will have dreadful torments; to whom so much is given, much will be required. How dreadful to have minister after minister, preacher after preacher, say, "Lord God, I preached, but they would not hear." Think of this, professors, and God make you possessors!

20 Centuries of Great Preaching; Volume 3 (Waco, TX: Word Books Publishing, 1974), p. 145.

O, I could preach myself dead; I could be glad to preach myself dead, if God would convert you!

20 Centuries of Great Preaching; Volume 3 (Waco, TX: Word Books Publishing, 1974), p. 146.

Stop, stop, O sinner! Turn ye, turn ye, O ye unconverted men, for the end of that way you are now walking in, however right it may seem in your blinded eyes, will be death, even eternal destruction both of body and soul. Make no longer tarrying, I say: at your peril I charge you, step not one step further on in your present walk. For how do you know, O man, but the next step you take may be into Hell. Death may seize you, judgment find you, and then the great gulf will be fixed between you and endless glory forever and ever. O think of these things, all ye that are unwilling to walk with God. Lay them to heart. Show yourselves men, and in the strength of Jesus say, Farewell, lust of the flesh, I will no more walk with thee! Farewell, lust of the eye, and pride of life! Farewell, carnal acquaintance and enemies of the cross, I will no more walk and be intimate with you! Welcome Jesus, welcome your word, welcome your ordinances, welcome your Spirit, welcome your people, I will henceforth walk with you.

20 *Centuries of Great Preaching; Volume 3* (Waco, TX: Word Books Publishing, 1974), p. 158.

You, therefore, who have been swearers and cursers, you, who have been harlots and drunkards, you, who have been thieves and robbers, you, who have hitherto followed the sinful pleasures and diversions of life, let me beseech you, by the mercies of God in Christ Jesus, that you would no longer continue therein, but that you would forsake your evil ways, and turn unto the Lord, for He waits to be gracious unto you. He is ready, He is willing to pardon you of all your sins; but do not expect Christ to pardon you of sin, when you run into it, and will not abstain from complying with the temptations. But if you will be persuaded to abstain from evil and choose the good, to return unto the Lord, and repent of your wickedness, He has promised He will abundantly pardon you, He will heal your back-slidings, and will love you freely. Resolve now this day to have done with your sins forever. Let your old ways and you be separated; you must resolve against it, for there can be no true repentance without a resolution to forsake it.

Whitefield's Sermons (Grand Rapids, MI: Christian Classics Ethereal Library). Sermon: "A Penitent Heart, the Best New Year's Gift."

I would speak, till I could speak no more, so I could but bring you to Christ.

Whitefield's Sermons (Grand Rapids, MI: Christian Classics Ethereal Library). Sermon: "A Penitent Heart, the Best New Year's Gift."

But, poor souls! many of you, perhaps, are not hungry. You do not feel yourselves halt, or maimed, or blind, and therefore you have no relish for this spiritual entertainment. Well, be not angry with me for calling you; be not offended if I weep over you, because you know not the day of your visitation. If I must appear in judgment as a swift witness against you, I must. But that thought chills my blood! I cannot bear it; I feel that I could lay down my life for you. But I am not willing to go without you. What say you, my dear friends? I would put the question to you once more, Will you taste of Christ's supper, or will you not? You shall all be welcome. There is milk at this feast for babes, as well as meat for strong men, and for persons of riper years. There is room and provision for high and low, rich and poor, one with another; and our Savior will thank you for coming. Amazing condescension! Astonishing love! The thought of it quite overcomes me. Help me, help me, O believers, to bless and praise him.

Whitefield's Sermons (Grand Rapids, MI: Christian Classics Ethereal Library). Sermon: "The Gospel Supper."

O sinners, did you but know how highly God intends to exalt those who humble themselves, and believe in Jesus, surely you would humble yourselves, at least beg of God to humble you. For it is He that must strike the rock of your hearts, and cause floods of contrite tears to flow therefrom. O that God would give this sermon such a commission, as He once gave to the rod of Moses! I would strike you through and through with the rod of His word, until each of you was brought to cry out with the poor Publican, "God be merciful to me a sinner.

Whitefield's Sermons (Grand Rapids, MI: Christian Classics Ethereal Library). Sermon: "The Pharisee and Publican."

───•◦•───

Would weeping, would tears prevail on you, I could wish my head were waters, and my eyes fountains of tears, that I might weep out every argument, and melt you into love. Would anything I could do or suffer, influence your hearts, I think I could bear to pluck out my eyes, or even to lay down my life for your sakes.

Whitefield's Sermons (Grand Rapids, MI: Christian Classics Ethereal Library). Sermon: "The Marriage of Cana."

───•◦•───

I am willing to go to prison or death for you; but I am not willing to go to Heaven without you. The love of Jesus Christ constrains me to lift up my voice like a trumpet. My heart is now full; out of the abundance of the love which I have for your precious and immortal souls, my mouth now speaks; and I could now not only continue my discourse until midnight, but I could speak until I could speak no more.

Whitefield's Sermons (Grand Rapids, MI: Christian Classics Ethereal Library). Sermon: "The Indwelling of the Spirit, the Common Privilege of All Believers."

───•◦•───

You will at death wish you had lived the life of the righteous, that you might have died his death. Be advised then; consider what is before you, Christ and the world, holiness and sin, life and death: choose now for yourselves; let your choice be made immediately, and let that choice be your dying choice.

Whitefield's Sermons (Grand Rapids, MI: Christian Classics Ethereal Library). Sermon: "A Penitent Heart, the Best New Year's Gift."

I will not let you go: I have wrestled with God for my hearers in private, and I must wrestle with you here in public.

Whitefield's Sermons (Grand Rapids, MI: Christian Classics Ethereal Library). Sermon: "The Holy Spirit Convincing the World of Sin, Righteousness, and Judgment"

Poor Christless souls! Do you know what a condition you are in? Why, you are lying in the wicked one, the devil; he rules in you, he walks and dwells in you, unless you dwell in Christ, and the Comforter is come into your hearts. And will you contentedly lie in that wicked one that devil? What wages will he give you? Eternal death. O that you would come to Christ! The free gift of God through Him is eternal life. He will accept of you even now, if you will believe in Him.

Whitefield's Sermons (Grand Rapids, MI: Christian Classics Ethereal Library). Sermon: "The Holy Spirit Convincing the World of Sin, Righteousness, and Judgment."

Come then, do not send me sorrowful away: do not let me have reason to cry out, O my leanness, my leanness! Do not let me go weeping into my closet, and say, "Lord, they will not believe my report; Lord, I have called them, and they will not answer. I am unto them as a very pleasant song, and as one that plays upon a pleasant instrument; but their hearts are running after the lust of the eye, the lust of the flesh, and the pride of life." Would you be willing that I should give such an account of you, or make such a prayer before God? And yet I must not only do so here, but appear in judgment against you hereafter, unless you will come to Christ. Once more therefore I entreat you to come.

Whitefield's Sermons (Grand Rapids, MI: Christian Classics Ethereal Library). Sermon: "The Holy Spirit Convincing the World of Sin, Righteousness, and Judgment."

How know you whether Jesus will call for you any more, before He calls you by death to judgment? Linger, O linger no longer. Fly, fly for your lives. Arise quickly, and ... come to Jesus.

Whitefield's Sermons (Grand Rapids, MI: Christian Classics Ethereal Library). Sermon: "The Resurrection of Lazarus."

Come, you dead, Christ-less, unconverted sinners, come and see the place where they laid the body of the deceased Lazarus; behold Him laid out, bound hand and foot with grave-clothes, locked up and stinking in a dark cave, with a great stone placed on the top of it! View him again and again; go nearer to him; be not afraid; smell him, ah! How he stinks. Stop there now, pause a while; and while you are gazing upon the corpse of Lazarus, give me leave to tell you with great plainness, but greater love, that this dead, bound, entombed, stinking carcass, is but a faint representation of your poor soul in its natural state. Whether you believe it or not, your spirit, which you bear about with you, sepulchered in flesh and blood, is as literally dead to God and as truly dead in trespasses and sins as the body of Lazarus was in the cave. Was he bound hand and foot with grave-clothes? So are you bound hand and foot with your corruptions: and as a stone was laid on the sepulcher, so is there a stone of unbelief upon your stupid heart. Perhaps you have lain in this state, not only for days, but many years, stinking in God's nostrils. And; what is still more affecting, you are as unable to raise yourself out of this loathsome, dead state, to a life of righteousness and true holiness, as ever Lazarus was to raise himself from the cave in which he lay so long.

You may try the power of your own boasted free-will, and the force and energy of moral persuasion and rational arguments (which, without all doubt, have their proper place in religion); but all your efforts, exerted with ever so much vigor, will prove quite fruitless and abortive, till that same

Jesus, who said, "Take away the stone," and cried, "Lazarus, come forth," comes by His mighty power, removes the stone of unbelief, speaks life to your dead soul, looses you from the fetters of your sins and corruptions, and by the influences of His blessed Spirit, enables you to arise, and to walk in the way of His holy commandments. And O that He would now rend the heavens, and come down amongst you! O that there may be a stirring among the dry bones this day! O that while I am speaking, and saying, "Dead sinners, come forth," a power, an almighty power might accompany the word, and cause you to emerge into new life!"

Whitefield's Sermons (Grand Rapids, MI: Christian Classics Ethereal Library). Sermon: "The Resurrection of Lazarus."

If the Lord should vouchsafe me such a mercy, and but one single soul in this great congregation, should arise and shake himself from the dust of his natural state; according to the present frame of my heart, I should not care if preaching this sermon here in the fields, was an occasion of hastening my death, as raising Lazarus hastened the death of my blessed Master. For I think death, in some respects, is more tolerable, than to see poor sinners, day by day, lying sepulchered, dead and stinking in sin. O that you saw how loathsome you are in the sight of God, while you continue in your natural state! I believe you would not so contentedly hug your chains, and refuse to be set at liberty.

Whitefield's Sermons (Grand Rapids, MI: Christian Classics Ethereal Library). Sermon: "The Resurrection of Lazarus."

How this flies in the face of modern preaching. — Ray Comfort

———•◦•———

O how could I weep over you, as our Lord wept over Jerusalem? For, alas! how distant must you be from God? What a prodigious work have you to finish, who, instead of praying day and night, seldom or never pray at all? And, instead of being born again of God, so as not to commit sin, are so deeply sunk into the nature of devils, as to make a mock at it? Or, instead of overcoming the world, so as not to follow or be led by it, are continually making provision for the flesh, to fulfill the lusts thereof. And, instead of being endued with the God-like disposition of loving all men, even your enemies, have your hearts full of hatred, malice, and revenge, and deride those who are the sincere followers of the lowly Jesus. But think you, O sinners, that God will admit such polluted wretches into His sight? Or should He admit you, do you imagine you could take any pleasure in Him? No; Heaven itself would be no Heaven to you; the devilish dispositions, which are in your hearts, would render all the spiritual enjoyments of those blessed mansions, ineffectual to make you happy. To qualify you to be blissful partakers of that heavenly inheritance with the saints in light, there is a meekness required: to attain which, ought to be the chief business of your lives.

Whitefield's Sermons (Grand Rapids, MI: Christian Classics Ethereal Library). Sermon: "Marks of Having Received the Holy Ghost."

------·•·------

Where are the scoffers of these last days, who count the lives of Christians to be madness, and their end to be without honor? Unhappy men! you know not what you do. Were your eyes open, and had you senses to discern spiritual things, you would not speak all manner of evil against the children of God, but you would esteem them as the excellent ones of the earth, and envy their happiness: your souls would hunger and thirst after it: you also would become fools for Christ's sake. You boast of wisdom; so did the philosophers of Corinth: but your wisdom is the foolishness of folly in the sight of God.

What will your wisdom avail you, if it does not make you wise unto salvation? Can you, with all your wisdom, propose a more consistent scheme to build you hopes of salvation on, than what has been now laid before you? Can you, with all the strength of natural reason, find out a better way of acceptance with God, than by the righteousness of the Lord Jesus Christ? Is it right to think your own works can in any measure deserve or procure it? If not, why will you not believe in Him? Why will you not submit to His righteousness? Can you deny that you are fallen creatures? Do not you find that you are full of disorders, and that these disorders make you unhappy? Do not you find that you cannot change your own hearts? Have you not resolved many and many a time, and have not your corruptions yet dominion over you? Are you not bond-slaves to your lusts, and led captive by the devil at his will? Why then will you not come to Christ for sanctification? Do you not desire to die the death of the righteous, and that your future state may be like theirs? I am persuaded you cannot bear the thoughts of being annihilated, much less of being miserable forever. Whatever you may pretend, if you speak truth, you must confess, that conscience breaks in upon you in more sober intervals whether you will or not, and even constrains you to believe that Hell is no painted fire. And why then will you not come to Christ? He alone can procure you everlasting redemption. Haste, haste away to Him, poor beguiled sinners. You lack wisdom; ask it of Christ. Who knows but He may give it to you? He is able for He is the wisdom of the Father. He is that wisdom which was from everlasting. You have no righteousness; away, therefore, to Christ: "He is the end of the law for righteousness to every one that believeth." You are unholy: flee to the Lord Jesus: He is full of grace and truth; and of His fullness all may receive that believe in Him. You are afraid to die; let this drive you to Christ. He has the keys of death and Hell: in Him is plenteous redemption; He alone can open the door which leads to everlasting life.

Whitefield's Sermons (Grand Rapids, MI: Christian Classics Ethereal Library). Sermon: "Christ, the Believer's Wisdom, Righteousness, Sanctification and Redemption."

Whatever you may think, it is the most unreasonable thing in the world not to believe on Jesus Christ, whom God has sent. Why, why will you die? Why will you not come unto Him, that you may have life? "Ho! everyone that thirsts, come to the waters of life, and drink freely: come, buy without money and without price." Were these blessed privileges in the text to be purchased with money, you might say, we are poor, and cannot buy: or, were they to be conferred only on sinners of such a rank or degree, then you might say, how can such sinners as we, expect to be so highly favored? But they are to be freely given of God to the worst of sinners. "To us," says the apostle, to me a persecutor, to you Corinthians, who were "unclean, drunkards, covetous persons, idolaters." Therefore, each poor sinner may say then, why not unto me?

Whitefield's Sermons (Grand Rapids, MI: Christian Classics Ethereal Library). Sermon: "Christ, the Believer's Wisdom, Righteousness, Sanctification and Redemption."

And as for you who ... proclaim your sin like Sodom, and willfully and daringly live without God in the world; I ask you, how can you think to escape, if you persist in neglecting such a great salvation? Verily, I should utterly despair of your ever attaining the blessed privilege of being temples of the living God, did I not hear of thousands, who through the grace of God have been translated from a like state of darkness into His marvelous light. Such, says the apostle Paul, writing to these very Corinthians who were now God's living temples, (drunkards, whoremongers, adulterers, and such like) "such were some of you. But ye are washed, but ye are sanctified, but ye are justified in the name of the Lord Jesus, and by the Spirit of our God.

O that the same blessed Spirit may this day vouchsafe to come and pluck you also as brands out of the burning! Behold,

I warn you to flee from the wrath to come. Go home, and meditate on these things; and think whether it is not infinitely better, even here, to be temples of the living God, than to be bond-slaves to every brutish lust, and to be led captive by the devil at his will.

The Lord Jesus can, and if you fly to Him for refuge, He will set your souls at liberty. He hath led captivity captive, he hath ascended up on high, on purpose to receive this gift of the blessed Spirit of God for men, "even for the rebellious," that He might dwell in your hearts by faith here, and thereby prepare you to dwell with Him and all the heavenly host in His kingdom hereafter.

Whitefield's Sermons (Grand Rapids, MI: Christian Classics Ethereal Library). Sermon: "Christians, Temples of the Living God."

———•••———

You had ten thousand times better be ignorant of all the polite diversions of the age, than to be ignorant of the spirit of Christ's being within you, and that it must be, before you are new creatures, and are in Christ. And if you have not an interest in Christ, you are lost; your damnation is hastening on. "He that believes shall be saved, and he that believes not shall be damned."

If you stand out against Christ, you are fighting against yourselves. O come unto Him, do not stay to bring good works with you, for they will be of no service; all your works will never carry you to Heaven, they will never pardon one sin, nor give you the least comfort in a dying hour. If you have nothing more than your own works to recommend you to God, they will not prevent your sinking in that eternal abyss, where there is no bottom.

But come unto Christ, and He will give you that righteousness which will stand you in good account at the great day of the

Lord, when He shall come to take notice of them that love Him, and of those who have the wedding garment on.

Whitefield's Sermons (Grand Rapids, MI: Christian Classics Ethereal Library). Sermon: "Christ the Only Preservative Against a Reprobate Spirit."

Therefore, my brethren, I beseech you, in the bowels of love and compassion, that you would come unto Jesus: Do not go away scoffing, offended, or blaspheming. Indeed, all I say is in love to your souls; and if I could be but an instrument of bringing you to Jesus Christ, if you were to be never so much exalted, I should not envy, but rejoice in your happiness. If I were to make up the last of the train of the companions of the blessed Jesus, it would rejoice me to see you above me in glory. I do not speak out of a false humility, a pretended sanctity; no, God is my judge, I speak the truth in Christ. I lie not, I would willingly go to prison, or to death for you, so I could but bring one soul from the devil's strong holds, into the salvation which is by Christ Jesus.

Whitefield's Sermons (Grand Rapids, MI: Christian Classics Ethereal Library). Sermon: "Christ the Only Preservative Against a Reprobate Spirit."

I offer Jesus Christ, pardon, and salvation to all you, who will accept thereof. Come, O you drunkards, lay aside your cups, drink no more to excess; come and drink of the water which Christ will give you, and then you will thirst no more. Come, O you thieves; let him that has stolen, steal no more, but fly unto Christ and He will receive you. Come unto Him, O you harlots; lay aside your lusts and turn unto the Lord, and He will have mercy upon you, He will cleanse you of all your sins, and wash you in His blood. Come, all you liars; come, all you Pharisees; come, all you fornicators, adulterers, swearers, and blasphemers, come to Christ, and He will take away all your filth. He will cleanse you from your pollution, and your sins shall be done away. Come, come, my guilty brethren; I beseech you for Christ's sake, and for your immortal soul's sake, to come unto Christ. Do not let me knock at the door of your hearts in vain, but open and let the King of Glory in, and He will dwell with you. He will come and sup with you this night; this hour, this moment He is ready to receive you, therefore come unto Him.

Whitefield's Sermons (Grand Rapids, MI: Christian Classics Ethereal Library). Sermon: "Christ the Only Preservative Against a Reprobate Spirit."

Do not consult with flesh and blood, let not the world hinder you from coming to the Lord of Life. What are a few transitory pleasures of this life worth? They are not worth your having, but Jesus Christ is a pearl of great price, He is worth the laying out all you have, to buy.

Whitefield's Sermons (Grand Rapids, MI: Christian Classics Ethereal Library). Sermon: "Christ the Only Preservative Against a Reprobate Spirit."

I think I could speak till midnight unto you, my brethren. I am full of love towards you; let me beseech you to fly to Christ for succor. "Now is the accepted time, now is the day of salvation." Therefore delay not, but strive to enter in at the strait gate; do not go the broad way of the polite world, but choose to suffer affliction with the people of God, rather than to enjoy the pleasures of sin for a season. You will have a reward afterwards that will make amends for all the taunts, jeers, and calamities you may undergo here.

And will not the presence of Christ be a sufficient reward for all you have suffered for His name's sake? Why will you not accept the Lord of glory? Do not say you have not heard of Christ, for he is now offered to you, and you will not accept of Him. Do not blame my master, He is willing to save you, if you will but lay hold on Him by faith; and if you do not, your blood will be required of your own heads.

But I hope that you will not let the blood of Jesus be shed in vain, and that you will not let my preaching be of no signification. Would you have me go and tell my Master, you will not come, and that I have spent my strength in vain; I cannot bear to carry so unpleasing a message unto Him. I would not, indeed. I would not be a swift witness against any of you at the great day of accounts. But if you will refuse these gracious invitations, and not accept of them, I must do it. And will it not move your tender hearts to see your friends taken up into Heaven, and you yourselves thrust down into Hell? But I hope better things of most of you, even that you will turn unto the Lord of Love, the Jesus who died for you, that in the day when He shall come to take His people to the mansions of everlasting rest, you may hear His voice, "Come, ye blessed of my Father, enter into the kingdom prepared for you before the foundation of the world.

Whitefield's Sermons (Grand Rapids, MI: Christian Classics Ethereal Library). Sermon: "Christ the Only Preservative Against a Reprobate Spirit."

——————•◦•——————

Give me leave to ask you, in the presence of God, whether you know the time, and if you do not know exactly the time, do you know there was a time, when God wrote bitter things against you, when the arrows of the Almighty were within you? Was ever the remembrance of your sins grievous to you? Was the burden of your sins intolerable to your thoughts? Did you ever see that God's wrath might justly fall upon you, on account of your actual transgressions against God? Were you ever in all your life sorry for your sins? Could you ever say, My sins are gone over my head as a burden too heavy for me to bear? Did you ever experience any such thing as this? Did ever any such thing as this pass between God and your soul? If not, for Jesus Christ's sake, do not call yourselves Christians. You may speak peace to your hearts, but there is no peace. May the Lord awaken you, may the Lord convert you, may the Lord give you peace.

Whitefield's Sermons (Grand Rapids, MI: Christian Classics Ethereal Library). Sermon: "The Method of Grace."

My business this morning, the first day of the week, is to tell you that Christ is willing to be reconciled to you. Will any of you be reconciled to Jesus Christ? Then, He will forgive you all your sins; He will blot out all your transgressions. But if you will go on and rebel against Christ, and stab him daily — if you will go on and abuse Jesus Christ, the wrath of God you must expect will fall upon you. God will not be mocked; that which a man sows, that shall he also reap. And if you will not be at peace with God, God will not be at peace with you. Who can stand before God when He is angry? It is a dreadful thing to fall into the hands of an angry God.

Whitefield's Sermons (Grand Rapids, MI: Christian Classics Ethereal Library). Sermon: " The Method of Grace."

Prayers for the Lost

Show them, O Father, wherein they have offended you; make them to see their own vileness, and that they are lost and undone without true repentance; and O give them that repentance, we beseech you, that they may turn from sin unto you the living and true God. These things, and whatever else you see needful for us, we entreat that you would bestow upon us, on account of what the dear Jesus Christ has done and suffered. To whom, with yourself, and holy Spirit, three persons, and one God, be ascribed, as is most due, all power, glory, might, majesty, and dominion, now, henceforth, and for evermore. Amen.

Whitefield's Sermons (Grand Rapids, MI: Christian Classics Ethereal Library). Sermon: "A Penitent Heart, the Best New Year's Gift."

Witnessing

Whatever opportunity you have, do it vigorously, do it speedily, do not defer it. If you see one hurrying on to destruction, use the utmost of your endeavor to stop him in his course. Show him the need he has of repentance, and that without it he is lost forever. Do not regard his despising of you; still go on to show him his danger: and if your friends mock and despise, do not let that discourage you. Hold on, hold out to the end, so you shall have a crown which is immutable, and that fades not away.

Whitefield's Sermons (Grand Rapids, MI: Christian Classics Ethereal Library). Sermon: "A Penitent Heart, the Best New Year's Gift."

We should, my dear brethren, use all means and opportunities for the salvation of our own souls, and of the souls of others. We may have a great deal of charity and concern for the bodies of our fellow-creatures, when we have no thought, or concern, for their immortal souls. But O how sad is it to have thought for a mortal, but not for the immortal part, to have charity for the body of our fellow-creatures while we have no concern for their immortal souls. It may be, we help them to ruin them, but have no concern in the saving of them.

You may love to spend a merry evening, to go to a play, or a horserace with them; but on the other hand, you cannot bear the thought of going to a sermon, or a religious society with them. No, you would sing the songs of the drunkard, but you will not sing hymns with them. This is not polite enough, this is unbecoming a gentleman of taste, unfashionable, and only practiced among a parcel of enthusiasts and madmen.

Thus, you will be so uncharitable as to join hand in hand with those who are hastening to their own damnation, while you will not be so charitable as to assist them in being brought from darkness to light, and from the power of Satan unto God. But this, this, my dear brethren, is the greatest charity, as can be, to save a soul from death. This is of far greater advantage than relieving the body of a fellow-creature: for the most miserable object as could be, death would deliver it from all. But death, to those who are not born again, would be so far from being a release from all misery, that it would be an inlet to all torment, and that to all eternity. Therefore, we should assist, as much as possible, to keep a soul from falling into the hands of Satan: for he is the grand enemy of souls. How should this excite you to watch over your own and others' souls? For unless you are earnest with God, Satan will be too hard for you. Surely, it is the greatest charity to watch over one another's words and actions, that we may forewarn each other when danger is nigh, or when the enemy of souls approaches.

Whitefield's Sermons (Grand Rapids, MI: Christian Classics Ethereal Library). Sermon: "The Great Duty of Charity Recommended."

And if you have once known the value of your own souls, and know what it is to be snatched as brands out of the burning fire, you will be solicitous that others may be brought out of the same state.

Whitefield's Sermons (Grand Rapids, MI: Christian Classics Ethereal Library). Sermon: "The Great Duty of Charity Recommended."

Consider, my dear brethren, that it was love for souls, that brought the blessed Jesus down from the bosom of His Father; that made Him, who was equal in power and glory, to come and take upon Him our nature; that caused the Lord of life to die the painful, ignominious, and accursed death of the cross. It was love to immortal souls that brought this blessed Jesus among us. And O that we might hence consider how great the value of souls was and is: it was that which made Jesus to bled, pant, and die. And surely souls must be of infinite worth, which made the Lamb of God to die so shameful a death.

And shall not this make you have a true value for souls? It is of the greatest worth: and this, this is the greatest charity, when it comes from love to God, and from love to souls. This will be a charity, the satisfaction of which will last to all eternity. O that this may make you have so much regard for the value of souls, as not to neglect all opportunities for the doing of them good: here is something worth having charity for, because they remain to all eternity. Therefore, let me earnestly beseech you both to consider the worth of immortal souls, and let your charity extend to them, that by your advice and admonition, you may be an instrument, in the hands of God, in bringing souls to the Lord Jesus.

Whitefield's Sermons (Grand Rapids, MI: Christian Classics Ethereal Library). Sermon: "The Great Duty of Charity Recommended."

It cannot be easy to see souls in the highway to destruction, and not use our utmost endeavor to bring them back from sin, and show them the dreadful consequence of running into evil. Christians cannot bear to see those souls for whom Christ died, perish for want of knowledge.

Whitefield's Sermons (Grand Rapids, MI: Christian Classics Ethereal Library). Sermon: "The Great Duty of Charity Recommended."

Open Air Preaching

Let not the adversaries say I have thrust myself out. No, they have thrust me out. And since the self-righteous men of this generation count themselves unworthy, I go out into the highways and hedges, and compel harlots, publicans, and sinners to come in, that my Master's house may be filled.

George Whitefield; God's Anointed Servant in the Great Revival of the Eighteenth Century, by Arnold A. Dallimore, (Wheaton, IL: Crossway Books, 1990), p. 50.

The whole world is my parish. Wherever my Master calls me, I am ready to go and preach the everlasting Gospel.

George Whitefield; God's Anointed Servant in the Great Revival of the Eighteenth Century, by Arnold A. Dallimore, (Wheaton, IL: Crossway Books, 1990), p. 66.

———•·•———

I could not bear, my brethren, to see you in the highway to destruction, and none to bring you back. It was love to your souls; it was a desire to see Christ formed in you, which brought me into the fields, the highways, and hedges, to preach unto you Jesus, a crucified Jesus as dying for you. It was charity, indeed it was charity to your souls.

Whitefield's Sermons (Grand Rapids, MI: Christian Classics Ethereal Library). Sermon: "The Great Duty of Charity Recommended."

———•·•———

First, we hear Moses' voice. We hear the voice of the Law. There is no going to Mount Zion but by the way of Mount Sinai. That is the right straight road. I know some say they do not know when they were converted. Those are, I believe, very few. Generally—no, I may say almost always—God deals otherwise. Some are, indeed, called sooner by the Lord than others, but before they are made to see the glory of God, they must hear the voice of the Law. So, too, you must hear the voice of the Law before you will ever be savingly called to God.

The World's Greatest Preachers, compiled by Ray Comfort and Kirk Cameron (New Kensington, PA: Whitaker House, 2003), p.81.

Believe me, I have been doing no more than you allow your bodily physicians to do every day: if you have a wound, and are in earnest about a cure, you bid the surgeon probe it to the very bottom. And shall not the physician of your souls be allowed the same freedom? What have I been doing but searching your natural wounds, that I might convince you of your danger, and put you upon applying to Jesus Christ for a remedy? Indeed I have dealt with you as gently as I could;

and now I have wounded, I will attempt to heal you ... This, this is what I long to come to. Hitherto I have been preaching only the law; but behold, I bring you glad tidings of great joy. If I have wounded you, be not afraid. Behold, I now bring a remedy for all your wounds. Notwithstanding, you are sunk into the nature of the beast and devil, yet, if you truly believe on Jesus Christ, you shall receive the quickening Spirit promised ... and be restored to the glorious liberties of the sons of God; I say, if you believe on Jesus Christ.

Whitefield's Sermons (Grand Rapids, MI: Christian Classics Ethereal Library). Sermon: "The Indwelling of the Spirit, the Common Privilege of All Believers."

———•◦•———

When our Lord was conversing with the woman of Samaria, He convinced her first of her adultery: "Woman, go call your husband. The woman answered, and said, I have no husband. Jesus said unto her, you have well said, I have no husband: for you have had five husbands, and he whom you now have, is not your husband: in this said you truly." With this, there went such a powerful conviction of all her other actual sins, that soon after she left her water-pot, and went her way into the city, and said to the men, "Come, and see a man that told me all things that ever I did: is not this the Christ?" Thus our Lord also dealt with the persecutor Saul: he convinced him first of the horrid sin of persecution; "Saul, Saul, why persecutest you me?" Such a sense of all his other sins, probably at the same time revived in his mind, that immediately he died; that is, died to all his false confidences, and was thrown into such an agony of soul, that he continued three days, and neither did eat nor drink. This is the method the Spirit of God generally takes in dealing with sinners; He first convinces them of some heinous actual sin, and at the same time brings all their other sins into remembrance, and as it were sets them in battle-array before them.

Whitefield's Sermons (Grand Rapids, MI: Christian Classics Ethereal Library). Sermon: "The Holy Spirit Convincing the World of Sin, Righteousness, and Judgment."

And if we are thus offenders against God, it follows, that we stand in need of forgiveness for thus offending Him; unless we suppose God to enact laws, and at the same time not care whether they are obeyed or no; which is as absurd as to suppose that a prince should establish laws for the proper government of his country, and yet let every violator of them come off with impunity. But God has not dealt so foolishly with His creatures. No, as He gave us a law, He demands our obedience to that law, and has obliged us universally and perseveringly to obey it, under no less a penalty than incurring His curse and eternal death for every breach of it. For thus speaks the scripture; "Cursed is he that continues not in all things that are written in the law to do them;" as the scripture also speaks in another place, "The soul that sinneth, it shall die." Now it has already been proved, that we have all of us sinned; and therefore, unless some means can be found to satisfy God's justice, we must perish eternally ... For surely nothing can well be supposed more deplorable ... but to be convicted as actual breakers of God's law, the least breach of which justly deserves eternal damnation ... O wretched men that we are! Who shall deliver us? I thank God, our Lord Jesus Christ ... there is no possibility of obtaining this justification, which we so much want, but by the all-perfect obedience and precious death of Jesus Christ.

Whitefield's Sermons (Grand Rapids, MI: Christian Classics Ethereal Library). Sermon: "Of Justification by Christ."

———•◦•———

God the Father awakens a sinner by the terrors of the Law, and by His Holy Spirit convinces him of sin, in order to lead him to Christ, and show him the necessity of a Redeemer.

Whitefield's Sermons (Grand Rapids, MI: Christian Classics Ethereal Library). Sermon: "Satan's Devices."

———•◦•———

The Law denounces threats against all who do not conform to her strict commands; but the gospel is a declaration of grace, peace and mercy. Here you have an account of the blood of Christ, blood that speaks better things than that of Abel, for Abel's blood cried aloud from vengeance, vengeance. But Jesus Christ's cried mercy, mercy, mercy upon the guilty sinner. If he comes to Christ, confesses and forsakes his sin, then Jesus will have mercy upon him. And if, my brethren, you are but sensible of your sins, convinced of your iniquities, and feel yourselves lost, undone sinners, and come and tell Christ of your lost condition, you will soon find how ready he is to help you.

Whitefield's Sermons (Grand Rapids, MI: Christian Classics Ethereal Library). Sermon: "Christ the Only Preservative Against a Reprobate Spirit."

Before you can speak peace to your hearts, you must be made to see, made to feel, made to weep over, made to bewail, your actual transgressions against the law of God... the least deviation from the moral law, according to the covenant of works, whether in thought, word, or deed, deserves eternal death at the hand of God. And if one evil thought, if one evil word, if one evil action, deserves eternal damnation, how many hells, my friends, do every one of us deserve, whose whole lives have been one continued rebellion against God! Before ever, therefore, you can speak peace to your hearts, you must be brought to see, brought to believe, what a dreadful thing it is to depart from the living God.

Whitefield's Sermons (Grand Rapids, MI: Christian Classics Ethereal Library). Sermon: " The Method of Grace."

The Conscience

Conscience, conscience, conscience, the candle of the Lord, may He help you to light a poor sinner into a knowledge of himself. I charge you in the name of our Lord Jesus Christ, in the name of that Savior, in whose name and by whose power, I trust I now preach; O conscience! You faithful monitor, let everyone hear their own. Come, if conscience was to speak what would it say? Why, that if you are not acquainted with yourself and Christ, you are lost forever.

20 Centuries of Great Preaching; Volume 3 (Waco, TX: Word Books Publishing, 1974), p. 125.

————

The care of the soul is the one thing needful, because, "without it you cannot secure the peace of your own mind, nor avoid the upbraiding of your conscience." That noble faculty is indeed the vicegerent of God in the soul. It is sensible of the dignity and worth of an immortal spirit, and will sometimes cry out of the violence that is offered to it, and cry so loud, as to compel the sinner to hear, whether he will or not.

Do you not sometimes find it yourselves? When you labor most to forget the concerns of your soul, do they not sometimes force themselves on your remembrance? You are afraid of the reflections of your own mind, but with all your artifice and all your resolution, can you entirely avoid them? Does not conscience follow you to your beds, even if denied the opportunity of meeting you in your closets, and, though with an unwelcome voice, there warn you, "that your soul is neglected, and will quickly be lost." Does it not follow you to your shops and your fields, when you are busiest there? Nay, I will add, does it not sometimes follow you to the feast, to the club, to the dance, and perhaps, amidst all resistance, to the theater too? Does, it not sometimes mingle your sweetest draughts with wormwood, and your gayest scenes with horror?

So that you are like a tradesman, who, suspecting his affairs to be in a bad posture, lays by his books and his papers, yet sometimes they will come accidentally in his way. He hardly dares to look abroad for fear of meeting a creditor or an arrest: and if he labors to forget his cares and his dangers, in a course of luxury at home, the remembrance is sometimes awakened, and the alarm increased, by those very extravagancies in which he is attempting to lose it. Such probably is the case of your minds, and it is a very painful state; and while things are thus within, external circumstances can no more make you happy, than a fine dress could relieve you under a violent fit of the stone. Whereas, if this great affair were secured, you might delight in reflection, as much as you now dread it; and conscience, of your bitterest enemy, would become a delightful friend, and the testimony of it your greatest rejoicing.

Whitefield's Sermons (Grand Rapids, MI: Christian Classics Ethereal Library). Sermon: "The Care of the Soul Urged as the One Thing Needful."

On Sin

The difference between one grain of sand and another, is not great, when it comes to be weighed against a talent of gold. Whatever it is, you had need to examine it carefully. You had need to view that commodity on all sides, of which you do in effect say, For this will I sell my soul; for this will I give up Heaven, and venture Hell, be heaven and Hell whatever they may. In the name of God, brethren, is this the part of a man, of a rational creature? To go on with your eyes open towards a pit of eternal ruin, because there are a few gay flowers in the way: or what if you shut your eyes, will that prevent your fall?

Whitefield's Sermons (Grand Rapids, MI: Christian Classics Ethereal Library). Sermon: "The Care of the Soul Urged as the One Thing Needful."

———•◦•———

Christ came to save such as are lost; and if you are enabled to groan under the weight and burden of your sins, then Christ will ease you and give you rest. And till you are thus sensible of your misery and lost condition, you are a servant to sin and to your lusts, under the bondage and command of Satan, doing his drudgery: you are under the curse of God, and liable to His judgment. Consider how dreadful your state will be at death, and after the day of judgment, when you will be exposed to such miseries which the ear has not heard, neither can the heart conceive, and that to all eternity, if you die impenitent.

Whitefield's Sermons (Grand Rapids, MI: Christian Classics Ethereal Library). Sermon: "A Penitent Heart, the Best New Year's Gift."

O be humbled, be humbled, I beseech you, for your sins. Having spent so many years in sinning, what can you do less, than be concerned to spend some hours in mourning and sorrowing for the same, and be humbled before God. Look back into your lives, call to mind your sins, as many as possible as you can, the sins of your youth, as well as of your riper years. See how you have departed from a gracious Father, and wandered in the way of wickedness, in which you have lost yourselves, the favor of God, the comforts of His Spirit, and the peace of your own consciences. Then go and beg pardon of the Lord, through the blood of the Lamb, for the evil you have committed, and for the good you have omitted. Consider, likewise, the heinousness of your sins.

See what very aggravating circumstances your sins are attended with, how you have abused the patience of God, which should have led you to repentance. And when you find your heart hard, beg of God to soften it, cry mightily to Him, and He will take away your stony heart, and give you a heart of flesh.

Resolve to leave all your sinful lusts and pleasures; renounce, forsake, and abhor your old sinful course of life, and serve God in holiness and righteousness all the remaining part of life. If you lament and bewail past sins, and do not forsake them, your repentance is in vain, you are mocking of God, and deceiving your own soul. You must put off the old man with his deeds, before you can put on the new man, Christ Jesus.

Whitefield's Sermons (Grand Rapids, MI: Christian Classics Ethereal Library). Sermon: "A Penitent Heart, the Best New Year's Gift."

Do not say, that your sins are too many and too great to expect to find mercy! No, be they ever so many, or ever so great, the blood of the Lord Jesus Christ will cleanse you from all sins. God's grace, my brethren, is free, rich, and sovereign. Manassah was a great sinner, and yet he was pardoned; Zaccheus was gone far from God, and went out to see Christ, with no other view but to satisfy his curiosity; and yet Jesus met him, and brought salvation to his house. Manassah was an idolater and murderer, yet he received mercy; the other was an oppressor and extortioner, who had gotten riches by fraud and deceit, and by grinding the faces of the poor: so did Matthew too, and yet they found mercy.

Have you been blasphemers and persecutors of the saints and servants of God? So was St. Paul, yet he received mercy: Have you been common harlots, filthy and unclean persons? So was Mary Magdalene, and yet she received mercy. Have you been a thief? The thief upon the cross found mercy. I despair of none of you, however vile and profligate you have been; I say, I despair of none of you, especially when God has had mercy on such a wretch as I am.

Remember the poor Publican, how he found favor with God, when the proud, self-conceited Pharisee, who, puffed up with his own righteousness, was rejected. And if you will go to Jesus, as the poor Publican did, under a sense of your own unworthiness, you shall find favor as he did: there is virtue enough in the blood of Jesus, to pardon greater sinners than He has yet pardoned. Then be not discouraged, but come unto Jesus, and you will find Him ready to help in all your distresses, to lead you into all truth, to bring you from darkness to light, and from the power of Satan to God.

Whitefield's Sermons (Grand Rapids, MI: Christian Classics Ethereal Library). Sermon: "A Penitent Heart, the Best New Year's Gift."

Repentance

When we consider how heinous and aggravating our offenses are, in the sight of a just and holy God, that they bring down His wrath upon our heads, and occasion us to live under His indignation; how ought we thereby to be deterred from evil, or at least engaged to study to repent thereof, and not commit the same again.

Whitefield's Sermons (Grand Rapids, MI: Christian Classics Ethereal Library). Sermon: "A Penitent Heart, the Best New Year's Gift."

Consider how hateful your ways are to God, while you continue in sin; how abominable you are unto Him, while you run into evil. You cannot be said to be Christians while you are hating Christ, and His people; true repentance will entirely change you, the bias of your souls will be changed, then you will delight in God, in Christ, in His Law, and in His people. You will then believe that there is such a thing as inward feeling, though now you may esteem it madness and enthusiasm. You will not then be ashamed of becoming fools for Christ's sake; you will not regard being scoffed at; it is not then their pointing after you and crying, "Here comes another troop of His followers," will dismay you. No, your soul will abhor such proceedings, the ways of Christ and His people will be your whole delight.

Whitefield's Sermons (Grand Rapids, MI: Christian Classics Ethereal Library). Sermon: "A Penitent Heart, the Best New Year's Gift."

Our sorrow and grief for sin, must not spring merely from a fear of wrath; for if we have no other ground but that, it proceeds from self-love, and not from any love to God; and if love to God is not the chief motive of your repentance, your repentance is in vain, and not to be esteemed true.

Whitefield's Sermons (Grand Rapids, MI: Christian Classics Ethereal Library). Sermon: "A Penitent Heart, the Best New Year's Gift."

You who never have truly repented of your sins, and never have truly forsaken your lusts, be not offended if I speak plain to you; for it is love, love to your souls, that constrains me to speak. I shall lay before you your danger, and the misery to which you are exposed, while you remain impenitent in sin. And O that this may be a means of making you fly to Christ for pardon and forgiveness. While your sins are not repented of, you are in danger of death, and if you should die, you would perish forever. There is no hope of any who live and die in their sins, but that they will dwell with devils and damned spirits to all eternity. And how do we know we shall live much longer: we are not sure of seeing our own habitations this night in safety. What mean you then being at ease and pleasure while your sins are not pardoned? As sure as ever the word of God is true, if you die in that condition, you are shut out of all hope and mercy forever, and shall pass into ceaseless and endless misery.

Whitefield's Sermons (Grand Rapids, MI: Christian Classics Ethereal Library). Sermon: "A Penitent Heart, the Best New Year's Gift."

———•◦•———

You are lost, undone, without Him; and if He is not glorified in your salvation, He will be glorified in your destruction; if He does not come and make His abode in your hearts, you must take up an eternal abode with the devil and his angels.

Whitefield's Sermons (Grand Rapids, MI: Christian Classics Ethereal Library). Sermon: "The Conversion of Zaccheus."

Self Righteousness

Our Lord denounced dreadful woes against the self-righteous Pharisees; so ministers must cut and hack them, and not spare, but say woe, woe, woe to all those that will not submit to the righteousness of Jesus Christ!

20 Centuries of Great Preaching; Volume 3 (Waco, TX: Word Books Publishing, 1974), p. 139.

———•◦•———

Hear this, all ye self-righteous, tremble, and behold your doom! a dreadful doom, more dreadful than words can express, or thought conceive! If you refuse to humble yourselves … I call Heaven and earth to witness against you this day, that God shall visit you with all His storms, and pour all the vials of His wrath upon your rebellious heads. You exalted yourselves here, and God shall abase you hereafter; you are as proud as the devil, and with devils shall you dwell to all eternity. "Be not deceived, God is not mocked;" He sees your hearts, He knows all things. And, notwithstanding you may come up to the temple to pray, your prayers are turned into sin, and you go down to your houses unjustified, if you are self-righteous; and do you know what it is to be unjustified? Why, if you are unjustified, the wrath of God abides upon you. You are in your blood; all the curses of the law belong to you: cursed are you when you go out, cursed are you when you come in; cursed are your thoughts, cursed are your words, cursed are your deeds. Everything you do, say, or think, from morning to night is only one continued series of sin. However highly you may be esteemed in the sight of men, however you may be honored with the uppermost seats in the synagogues, in the church militant, you will have no place in the church triumphant. "Humble yourselves therefore under the mighty hand of God:" Pull down every self-righteous thought and every proud imagination, that now exalts itself against the perfect, personal, imputed righteousness of the dear Lord Jesus.

Whitefield's Sermons (Grand Rapids, MI: Christian Classics Ethereal Library). Sermon: "The Pharisee and Publican."

————•◦•————

We all naturally are Legalists, thinking to be justified by the works of the Law. When somewhat awakened by the terrors of the Lord, we immediately, like the Pharisees of old, go about to establish our own righteousness, and think we shall find acceptance with God, if we seek it with tears. Finding ourselves damned by nature and our actual sins, we then think to recommend ourselves to God by our duties, and hope, by our doings of one kind or another, to inherit eternal life. But, whenever the Comforter comes into the heart, it convinces the soul of these false rests, and makes the sinner so see that all his righteousnesses are but filthy rags. And that, for the most pompous services, he deserves no better a doom than that of the unprofitable servant, "to be thrown into outer darkness, where is weeping, and wailing, and gnashing of teeth."

And was this degree of conviction ever wrought in any of your souls? Did the Comforter ever come into your hearts, so as to make you sick of your duties, as well as your sins? Were you ever, with the great Apostle of the Gentiles, made to abhor your own righteousness, which is by the Law, and acknowledge that you deserve to be damned, though you should give all your goods to feed the poor? Were you made to feel, that your very repentance needed to be repented of, and that everything in yourselves is but dung and dross? And that all the arguments you can fetch for mercy, must be out of the heart and pure unmerited love of God? Were you ever made to lie at the feet of ... grace, and to say, Lord, if You will, You may save me; if not, You may justly damn me? I have nothing to plead; I can in no wise justify myself in Your sight. My best performances, I see, will condemn me; and all I have to depend upon is your free grace.

Whitefield's Sermons (Grand Rapids, MI: Christian Classics Ethereal Library). Sermon: "The Holy Spirit Convincing the World of Sin, Righteousness, and Judgment."

———•◦•———

It is true, such men are almost good; but almost to hit the mark, is really to miss it. God requires us "to love Him with all our hearts, with all our souls, and with all our strength." He loves us too well to admit any rival, because, so far as our hearts are empty of God, so far must they be unhappy. The devil, indeed, like the false mother that came before Solomon, would have our hearts divided, as she would have had the child; but God, like the true mother, will have all or none. "My Son, give me your heart," your whole heart, is the general call to all: and if this be not done, we never can expect the divine mercy.

Whitefield's Sermons (Grand Rapids, MI: Christian Classics Ethereal Library). Sermon: "The Almost Christian."

———•◦•———

A little acquaintance with the world will furnish us with instances, of no small number of persons, who, perhaps, were before openly profane. But seeing the ill consequences of their vices, and the many worldly inconveniencies it has reduced them to, on a sudden, as it were, grow civilized; and thereupon flatter themselves that they are very religious, because they differ a little from their former selves, and are not so scandalously wicked as once they were. Whereas, at the same time, they shall have some secret darling sin or other, some beloved Delilah or Herodias, which they will no part with; some hidden lust, which they will not mortify; some vicious habit, which they will not take pains to root out. But would you know, O vain man! Whoever you are, what the Lord your God requires of you? You must be informed, that nothing short of a thorough sound conversion will fit you for the kingdom of Heaven. It is not enough to turn from profaneness to civility; but you must turn from civility to godliness. Not only some, but "all things must become new" in your soul. It will profit you but little to do many things, if yet some one thing you lack. In short, you must not only be an almost, but altogether a new creature, or in vain you boast that you are a Christian.

Whitefield's Sermons (Grand Rapids, MI: Christian Classics Ethereal Library). Sermon: "On Regeneration."

―――•◦•―――

Awake therefore, you deceived formalists, awake; who, vainly puffed up with your model of performances, boastingly cry out, "The temple of the Lord, the temple of the Lord, the temple of the Lord we are." Awake, you outward-court worshippers: you are building on a sandy foundation. Take heed lest you also go to Hell by the very door of Heaven.

Whitefield's Sermons (Grand Rapids, MI: Christian Classics Ethereal Library). Sermon: "Christians, Temples of the Living God."

Jesus Christ

J esus Christ must be your whole wisdom, Jesus Christ must
be your whole righteousness, Jesus Christ must be your
whole sanctification, or He will never be your eternal
redemption.

Whitefield's Sermons (Grand Rapids, MI: Christian Classics Ethereal Library). Sermon: "A
Penitent Heart, the Best New Year's Gift."

Come, all of you, come, and behold Him stretched out for
you; see His hands and feet nailed to the cross. O come,
come, my brethren, and nail your sins thereto; come, come
and see His side pierced; there is a fountain open for sin,
and for uncleanness. O wash, wash and be clean. Come
and see His head crowned with thorns, and all for you. Can
you think of a panting, bleeding, dying Jesus, and not be
filled with pity towards Him? He underwent all this for you.
Come unto Him by faith; lay hold on Him: there is mercy for
every soul of you that will come unto Him. Then do not
delay; fly unto the arms of this Jesus, and you shall be made
clean in His blood.

Whitefield's Sermons (Grand Rapids, MI: Christian Classics Ethereal Library). Sermon: "A
Penitent Heart, the Best New Year's Gift."

———•◦•———

There, there, by faith, O mourners in Zion, may you see your
Savior hanging with arms stretched out, and hear Him, as it
were, thus speaking to your souls; "Behold how I have loved
you! Behold my hands and my feet! Look, look into my
wounded side, and see a heart flaming with love: love stronger
than death. Come into my arms, O sinners; come wash your
spotted souls in my heart's blood. See here is a fountain
opened for all sin and all uncleanness! See, O guilty souls,
how the wrath of God is now abiding upon you: come, haste
away, and hide yourselves in the clefts of my wounds; for I

am wounded for your transgressions; I am dying that you may live for evermore. Behold, as Moses lifted up the serpent in the wilderness, so am I here lifted up upon a tree. See how I am become a curse for you: the chastisement of your peace is upon me. I am thus scourged, thus wounded, thus crucified, that you by my stripes may be healed. O look unto me, all you trembling sinners, even to the ends of the earth! Look unto me by faith, and you shall be saved: for I came thus to be obedient even unto death, that I might save that which was lost."

Whitefield's Sermons (Grand Rapids, MI: Christian Classics Ethereal Library). Sermon: "The Conversion of Zaccheus."

We are freely justified by the death and obedience of Jesus Christ, let us here pause a while; and as before we have reflected on the misery of a fallen, let us now turn aside and see the happiness of the believing soul. But alas! how am I lost to think that God the Father, when we were in a state of enmity and rebellion against Him, should notwithstanding yearn in His bowels towards us His fallen, His apostate creatures: And because nothing but an infinite ransom could satisfy an infinitely offended justice, that should send His only and dear Son Jesus Christ (who is God, blessed forever, and who had lain in His bosom from all eternity) to fulfill the covenant of works, and die a cursed, painful, ignominious death, for us and for our salvation! Who can avoid crying out, at the consideration of His mystery of godliness? "Oh the depth of the riches of God's love" to us His wretched, miserable and undone creatures!

Whitefield's Sermons (Grand Rapids, MI: Christian Classics Ethereal Library). Sermon: "Of Justification by Christ."

As we admire the Father sending, let us likewise humbly and thankfully adore the Son coming, when sent to die for man. But O what thoughts can conceive, what words express the infinite greatness of that unparalleled love, which engaged the Son of God to come down from the mansions of His Father's glory to obey and die for sinful man! The Jews, when He only shed a tear at poor Lazarus' funeral, said, "Behold how He loved him." How much more justly then may we cry out, Behold how He loved us! When He not only fulfilled the whole moral Law, but did not spare to shed His own most precious blood for us.

Whitefield's Sermons (Grand Rapids, MI: Christian Classics Ethereal Library). Sermon: "Of Justification by Christ."

Can any poor truly-convicted sinner ... despair of mercy? What, can they see their Savior hanging on a tree, with arms stretched out ready to embrace them, and yet, on their truly believing on Him, doubt of finding acceptance with Him? No, away with all such dishonorable, desponding thoughts. Look on His hands, bored with pins of iron; look on His side, pierced with a cruel spear, to let loose the sluices of His blood, and open a fountain for sin, and for all uncleanness; and then despair of mercy if you can! No, only believe in Him, and then, though you have crucified Him afresh, yet will He abundantly pardon you.

Whitefield's Sermons (Grand Rapids, MI: Christian Classics Ethereal Library). Sermon: "Of Justification by Christ."

Now as man had sinned, and a satisfaction was demanded, it was impossible for a finite creature to satisfy Him, who was a God of such strict purity as not to behold iniquity. And man, by the justice of God, would have been sent down into the pit, which was prepared of old for the devil and his angels; but when justice was going to pass the irrevocable sentence, then the Lord Jesus Christ came and offered Himself a ransom for poor sinners. Here was admirable condescension of the Lord Jesus Christ! That He who was in the bosom of His father, should come down from all that glory, to die for such rebels as you and I are, who if it lay in our power, would pull the Almighty from His throne. Now can you think that if there was no need of Christ's death, can you think that if there could have been any other ransom found, whereby poor sinners might have been saved, God would not have spared his only begotten Son, and not have delivered him up for all that believe in Him?

Whitefield's Sermons (Grand Rapids, MI: Christian Classics Ethereal Library). Sermon: "Christ, the Only Preservative Against a Reprobate Spirit."

The Cross

O my friend! We can make no atonement to a violated Law— we have no inward holiness of our own—the Lord Jesus is the Lord our righteousness.

Cling not to such beggarly elements—such filthy rags—mere cob webs of Pharisaical pride—but look to Him who has wrought out a perfect righteousness for His people.

You find it a hard task to come naked and miserable to Christ … But if you come at all you must come thus … There must be no conditions—Christ and Christ alone must be the only Mediator between God and sinful men—no miserable performances may be placed between the sinner and the Savior. Let the eye of faith be ever directed to the Lord Jesus Christ; and I beseech Him to bring every thought of your heart into captivity to the obedience of our Great High Priest."

George Whitefield; God's Anointed Servant in the Great Revival of the Eighteenth Century, by Arnold A. Dallimore (Wheaton, IL: Crossway Books, 1990), p. 161.

Whoever know themselves and God, must acknowledge, that "Jesus Christ is the end of the law for righteousness, (and perfect justification in the sight of God) to everyone that believes," and that we are to be made the righteousness of God in Him. This, and this only, a poor sinner can lay hold of, as a sure anchor of his hope. Whatever other scheme of salvation men may lay, I acknowledge I can see no other foundation whereon to build my hopes of salvation, but on the rock of Christ's personal righteousness, imputed to my soul.

Whitefield's Sermons (Grand Rapids, MI: Christian Classics Ethereal Library). Sermon: "The Holy Spirit Convincing the World of Sin, Righteousness, and Judgment."

—————•◦•—————

They are enabled to lay hold on Christ by faith, and God the Father blots out their transgressions, as with a thick cloud their sins and their iniquities He remembers no more. They are made the righteousness of God in Christ Jesus, "who is the end of the law for righteousness to every one that believeth." In one sense, God now sees no sin in them; the whole covenant of works is fulfilled in them; they are actually justified, acquitted, and looked upon as righteous in the sight of God. They are perfectly accepted in the beloved; they are complete in Him; the flaming sword of God's wrath, which before moved every way, is not removed, and free access given to the tree of life. They are enabled to reach out the arm of faith, and pluck, and live for evermore. Hence it is that the apostle, under a sense of this blessed privilege, breaks out into this triumphant language; "It is Christ that justifies, who is he that condemns?" Does sin condemn? Christ's righteousness delivers believers from the guilt of it: Christ is their Savior, and is become a propitiation for their sins. Who therefore shall lay any thing to the charge of God's elect? Does the law condemn? By having Christ's righteousness imputed to them, they are dead to the law, as a covenant of works. Christ has fulfilled it for them, and in their stead. Does death threaten them? They need not fear: the sting of death is sin, the strength of sin is the law; but God has given them the victory by imputing to them the righteousness of the Lord Jesus.

Whitefield's Sermons (Grand Rapids, MI: Christian Classics Ethereal Library). Sermon: "Christ, the Believer's Wisdom, Righteousness, Sanctification and Redemption."

For it is not the greatness or number of our crimes, but impenitence and unbelief, that will prove our ruin. No, were our sins more in number than the hairs of our head, or of a deeper die than the brightest scarlet; yet the merits of the death of Jesus Christ are infinitely greater. And faith in His blood shall make them white as snow.

Whitefield's Sermons (Grand Rapids, MI: Christian Classics Ethereal Library). Sermon: "Satan's Devices."

Before we can ever have peace with God, we must be justified by faith through our Lord Jesus Christ. We must be enabled to apply Christ to our hearts, we must have Christ brought home to our souls, so as His righteousness may be made our righteousness, so as His merits may be imputed to our souls. My dear friends, were you ever married to Jesus Christ? Did Jesus Christ ever give Himself to you? Did you ever close with Christ by a lively faith, so as to feel Christ in your hearts, so as to hear Him speaking peace to your souls? Did peace ever flow in upon your hearts like a river? Did you ever feel that peace that Christ spoke to His disciples? I pray God may come and speak peace to you.

Whitefield's Sermons (Grand Rapids, MI: Christian Classics Ethereal Library). Sermon: "The Method of Grace."

Conversion

When our Lord says, we must be converted and become as little children, I suppose He means also, that we must be sensible of our weakness, comparatively speaking, as a little child.

What is conversion? ... man must be a new creature, and converted from his own righteousness to the righteousness of the Lord Jesus Christ. Conviction will always precede spiritual conversion, therefore the Protestant divines make this distinction; you may be convinced and not converted, but you cannot be converted without being convinced. And if we are truly converted, we shall not only be turned and converted from sinful self, but we shall be converted from righteous self; that is the devil of devils.

20 Centuries of Great Preaching; Volume 3 (Waco, TX: Word Books Publishing, 1974), p. 139.

In vain we may talk of being converted till we are bought out of ourselves; to come as poor lost undone sinners, to the Lord Jesus Christ; to be washed in His blood; to be clothed in His glorious imputed righteousness. The consequence of this imputation, or application of a Mediator's righteousness to the soul, will be a conversion from sin to holiness.

20 Centuries of Great Preaching; Volume 3 (Waco, TX: Word Books Publishing, 1974), p. 140.

———•◦•———

You do not love Christ, because you do not know Him. You do not come to Him, because you do not feel your want of Him: you are whole, and not broken hearted; you are not sick, at least not sensible of your sickness; and, therefore, no wonder you do not apply to Jesus Christ, that great, that almighty physician. You do not feel yourselves lost, and therefore do not seek to be found in Christ. O that God would wound you with the sword of His Spirit, and cause His arrows of conviction to stick deep in your hearts! O that He would dart a ray of divine light into your souls! For if you do not feel yourselves lost without Christ, you are of all men most miserable. Your souls are dead; you are not only an image of Hell, but in some degree Hell itself: you carry Hell about with you, and you know it not. O that I could see some of you sensible of this, and hear you cry out, "Lord, break this hard heart; Lord, deliver me from the body of this death; draw me, Lord, make me willing to come after you; I am lost; Lord, save me, or I perish!

Whitefield's Sermons (Grand Rapids, MI: Christian Classics Ethereal Library). Sermon: "The Conversion of Zaccheus."

———————•◦•———————

O what a privilege is this! to be changed from beasts into saints, and from a devilish, to be made partakers of a divine nature; to be translated from the kingdom of Satan, into the kingdom of God's dear Son! To put off the old man, which is corrupt, and to put on the new man, which is created after God, in righteousness and true holiness! O what an unspeakable blessing is this! I almost stand amazed at the contemplation thereof. Well might the apostle exhort believers to rejoice in the Lord; indeed they have reason always to rejoice, yea, to rejoice on a dying bed; for the kingdom of God is in them; they are changed from glory to glory, even by the Spirit of the Lord: well may this be a mystery to the natural, for it is a mystery even to the spiritual man himself, a mystery which he cannot fathom.

Does it not often dazzle your eyes, O you children of God, to look at your own brightness, when the candle of the Lord shines out, and your redeemer lifts up the light of His blessed countenance upon your souls? Are not you astonished, when you feel the love of God shed abroad in your hearts by the Holy Ghost, and God holds out the golden scepter of His mercy, and bids you ask what you will, and it shall be given you? Does not that peace of God, which keeps and rules your hearts, surpass the utmost limits of your understandings? And is not the joy you feel unspeakable? Is it not full of glory? I am persuaded it is; and in your secret communion, when the Lord's love flows in upon your souls, you are as it were swallowed up in, or, to use the apostle's phrase, "filled with all the fullness of God." Are not you ready to cry out with Solomon? "And will the Lord, indeed, dwell thus with men?" How is it that we should be thus your sons and daughters, O Lord God Almighty!

Whitefield's Sermons (Grand Rapids, MI: Christian Classics Ethereal Library). Sermon: "Christ, the Believer's Wisdom, Righteousness, Sanctification and Redemption."

———•◦•———

Let each of us therefore seriously put this question to our hearts: Have we received the Holy Ghost since we believed? Are we new creatures in Christ, or no? At least, if we are not so yet, is it our daily endeavor to become such? Do we constantly and conscientiously use all the means of grace required thereto? Do we fast, watch and pray? Do we, not lazily seek, but laboriously strive to enter in at the strait gate? In short, do we renounce our own righteousness, take up our crosses and follow Christ? If so, we are in that narrow way which leads to life; the good seed is sown in our hearts, and will, if duly watered and nourished by a regular persevering use of all the means of grace, grow up to eternal life. But on the contrary, if we have only heard, and know not experimentally, whether there be any Holy Ghost; if we are strangers to fasting, watching and prayer, and all the other spiritual exercises of devotion; if we are content to go in the broad way, merely because we see most other people do so, without once reflecting whether it be the right one or not; in short, if we are strangers, nay enemies to the cross of Christ, by lives of worldly-mindedness, and sensual pleasure, and thereby make others think, that Christianity is but an empty name, a bare formal profession; if this be the case, I say, Christ is as yet dead in vain, to us; we are under the guilt of our sins; and are unacquainted with a true and thorough conversion.

Whitefield's Sermons (Grand Rapids, MI: Christian Classics Ethereal Library). Sermon: "On Regeneration."

Indeed, was there no other reward attended a thorough conversion, but that peace of God, which is the unavoidable consequence of it, and which, even in this life, "passes all understanding," we should have great reason to rejoice. But when we consider, that this is the least of those mercies God has prepared for those that are in Christ, and become new creatures. That this is but the beginning of an eternal succession of pleasures. That the day of our deaths, which the unconverted, unrenewed sinner must so much dread, will be, as it were, but the first day of our new births, and open to us an everlasting scene of happiness and comfort. In short, if we remember, that they who are regenerate and born again, have a real title to all the glorious promises of the gospel, and are infallibly certain of being as happy, both here and hereafter, as an all-wise, all-gracious, all-powerful God can make them. I think, everyone that has but the least concern for the salvation of his precious and immortal soul, having such promises, such an hope, such an eternity of happiness set before him, should never cease watching, praying, and striving, till he finds a real, inward, saving change wrought in his heart. And thereby does know of a truth, that he dwells in Christ, and Christ in him; that he is a new creature, therefore a child of God; that he is already an inheritor, and will ere long be an actual possessor of the kingdom of Heaven.

Whitefield's Sermons (Grand Rapids, MI: Christian Classics Ethereal Library). Sermon: "On Regeneration."

Before you can speak peace to your hearts, you must not only be troubled for the sins of your life, the sin of your nature, but likewise for the sins of your best duties and performances. When a poor soul is somewhat awakened by the terrors of the Lord, then the poor creature, being born under the covenant of works, flies directly to a covenant of works again. And as Adam and Eve hid themselves among the trees of the garden, and sewed fig leaves together to cover their nakedness, so the poor sinner, when awakened, flies to his duties and to his performances, to hide himself from God, and goes to patch up a righteousness of his own. Says he, I will be mighty good now—I will reform—I will do all I can; and then certainly Jesus Christ will have mercy on me. But before you can speak peace to your heart, you must be brought to see that God may damn you for the best prayer you ever put up. You must be brought to see that all your duties—all your righteousness—as the prophet elegantly expresses it—put them all together, are so far from recommending you to God, are so far from being any motive and inducement to God to have mercy on your poor soul, that He will see them to be filthy rags, a menstruous cloth— that God hates them, and cannot away with them, if you bring them to him in order to recommend you to His favor.

Once more then: before you can speak peace to your heart, you must not only be convinced of your actual and original sin, the sins of your own righteousness, the sin of unbelief, but you must be enabled to lay hold upon the perfect righteousness, the all-sufficient righteousness, of the Lord Jesus Christ. You must lay hold by faith on the righteousness of Jesus Christ, and then you shall have peace. "Come," says Jesus, "unto me, all ye that are weary and heavy laden, and I will give you rest." This speaks encouragement to all that are weary and heavy laden. But the promise of rest is made to them only upon their coming and believing, and taking Him to be their God and their all.

Whitefield's Sermons (Grand Rapids, MI: Christian Classics Ethereal Library). Sermon: "The Method of Grace."

———•·•———

Let me exhort you ... to consider the love of the Lord Jesus Christ. O do not forget this love. Consider, I beseech you, how great it has been unto you, and do not slight this. His grace, the riches, the love, the kindness of your dear Redeemer, the Lord Jesus Christ, who has prepared this eternal rest for you. He also laid down His life for your sakes: what great love was here! That while you were enemies to the Lord of glory, He died for you, to redeem you from sin, from Hell and wrath, that you might live and reign with Him, world without end.

Whitefield's Sermons (Grand Rapids, MI: Christian Classics Ethereal Library). Sermon: "An Exhortation to the People of God Not to Be Discouraged in Their Way, by the Scoffs and Contempt of Wicked Men."

The End of the Day of Grace

O the folly and madness of this sensual world; sure if there were nothing in sin but present slavery, it would keep an ingenuous spirit from it. But to do the devil's drudgery! And if we do that, we shall have his wages, which is eternal death and condemnation; O consider this, my guilty brethren, you that think it no crime to swear, whore, drink, or scoff and jeer at the people of God; consider how your voices will then be changed, and you that counted their lives madness, and their end without honor, shall howl and lament at your own madness and folly, that should bring you to so much woe and distress. Then you will lament and bemoan your own dreadful condition; but it will be of no signification: for He that is not your merciful Savior, will then become your inexorable Judge. Now He is easy to be entreated; but then, all your tears and prayers will be in vain: for God has allotted to every man a day of grace, a time of repentance, which if he does not improve, but neglects and despises the means which are offered to him, he cannot be saved. *Whitefield's Sermons* (Grand Rapids, MI: Christian Classics Ethereal Library). Sermon: "A Penitent Heart, the Best New Year's Gift."

⁂

Judgment Day

I am content to wait till the Judgment Day for the clearing up of my reputation; and after I am dead, I desire no other epitaph then this, "Here lies G.W. What sort of man he was the great day will discover."

George Whitefield; God's Anointed Servant in the Great Revival of the Eighteenth Century, by Arnold A. Dallimore, (Wheaton, IL: Crossway Books, 1990), p. 154.

What horror and astonishment will possess your souls? Then all your lies and oaths, your scoffs and jeers at the people of God, all your filthy and unclean thoughts and actions, your misspent time in balls, plays, and assemblies, your spending whole evenings at cards, dice, and masquerades, your frequenting of taverns and alehouses, your worldliness, covetousness, and your uncharity, will be brought at once to your remembrance, and at once charged upon your guilty soul. And how can you bear the thoughts of these things? Indeed I am full of compassion towards you, to think that this should be the portion of any who now hear me. These are truths, though awful ones; my brethren, these are the truths of the gospel; and if there was not a necessity for thus speaking, I would willingly forbear: for it is no pleasing subject to me, any more than it is to you; but it is my duty to show you the dreadful consequences of continuing in sin. I am only now acting the part of a skillful surgeon, who searches a wound before he heals it. I would show you your danger first, that deliverance may be the more readily accepted by you.

Whitefield's Sermons (Grand Rapids, MI: Christian Classics Ethereal Library). Sermon: "A Penitent Heart, the Best New Year's Gift."

Consider, that however you may be for putting the evil day away from you, and are now striving to hide your sins, at the Day of Judgment there shall be a full discovery of all. Hidden things on that day shall be brought to light; and after all your sins have been revealed to the whole world, then you must depart into everlasting fire in Hell, which will not be quenched night and day; it will be without intermission, without end. O then, what stupidity and senselessness have possessed your hearts, that you are not frightened from your sins. The fear of Nebuchadnezzar's fiery furnace, made men do any thing to avoid it; and shall not an everlasting fire make men, make you, do any thing to avoid it? O that this would awaken and cause you to humble yourselves for your sins, and to beg pardon for them, that you might find mercy in the Lord.

Whitefield's Sermons (Grand Rapids, MI: Christian Classics Ethereal Library). Sermon: "A Penitent Heart, the Best New Year's Gift."

Let me beseech you to cast away your transgressions, to strive against sin, to watch against it, and to beg power and strength from Christ, to keep down the power of those lusts that hurry you on in your sinful ways. But if you will not do any of these things, if you are resolved to sin on, you must expect eternal death to be the consequence. You must expect to be seized with horror and trembling, with horror and amazement, to hear the dreadful sentence of condemnation pronounced against you. And then you will run and call upon the mountains to fall on you, to hide you from the Lord, and from the fierce anger of His wrath. Had you now a heart to turn from your sins unto the living God, by true and unfeigned repentance, and to pray unto Him for mercy, in and through the merits of Jesus Christ, there were hope.

But at the Day of Judgment, your prayers and tears will be of no signification. They will be of no service to you, the Judge will not be entreated by you: as you would not hearken to Him when He called unto you, but despised both Him and His ministers, and would not leave your iniquities. Therefore, on that day He will not be entreated, notwithstanding all your cries and tears. For God Himself has said, "Because I have called, and you refused; I have stretched out my hand, and no man regarded, but ye have set at nought all my counsel, and would have one of my reproof; I will also laugh at your calamity, and mock when your fear cometh as desolation, and your destruction cometh as a whirlwind. When distress and anguish cometh upon you, then shall they call upon me, but I will not answer, they shall seek me early, but they shall not find me."

Now you may call this enthusiasm and madness; but at that great day, if you repent not of your sins here, you will find, by woeful experience, that your own ways were madness indeed. But God forbid it should be left undone till then: seek after the Lord while He is to be found; call upon Him while He is near, and you shall find mercy: repent this hour, and Christ will joyfully receive you.

Whitefield's Sermons (Grand Rapids, MI: Christian Classics Ethereal Library). Sermon: "A Penitent Heart, the Best New Year's Gift."

I may never see your faces again; but at the Day of Judgment I will meet you. There you will either bless God that ever you were moved to repentance; or else this sermon, though in a field, will be as a swift witness against you. Repent, repent therefore, my dear brethren, as John the Baptist, and as our blessed Redeemer Himself earnestly exhorted, and turn from your evil ways, and the Lord will have mercy on you.

Whitefield's Sermons (Grand Rapids, MI: Christian Classics Ethereal Library). Sermon: "A Penitent Heart, the Best New Year's Gift."

I think I see the poor wretches dragged out of their graves by the devil; I think I see them trembling, crying out to the hills and rocks to cover them. But the devil will say, Come, I will take you away; and then they shall stand trembling before the judgment-seat of Christ. They shall appear before Him to see Him once, and hear Him pronounce that irrevocable sentence, "Depart from me, ye cursed." I think I hear the poor creatures saying, Lord, if we must be damned, let some angel pronounce the sentence. No, the God of Love, Jesus Christ, will pronounce it. Will you not believe this? Do not think I am talking at random, but agreeably to the Scriptures of Truth. If you do not, then show yourselves men, and this morning go away with full resolution, in the strength of God, to cleave to Christ. And may you have no rest in your souls till you rest in Jesus Christ!

Whitefield's Sermons (Grand Rapids, MI: Christian Classics Ethereal Library). Sermon: "The Method of Grace."

Some talk of being justified at the Day of Judgment; that is nonsense; if we are not justified here, we shall not be justified there.

Whitefield's Sermons (Grand Rapids, MI: Christian Classics Ethereal Library). Sermon: "The Good Shepherd: A Farewell Sermon."

Fear of Death

Have you never seen a gay, thoughtless creature, surprised in the giddy round of pleasures and amusements, and presently brought not only to seriousness, but terror and trembling, by the near views of death? Have you never seen the man of business and care interrupted, like the rich fool in the parable, in the midst of his schemes for the present world? And have you not heard one and the other of them owning the vanity of those pleasures and cares, which but a few days ago were everything to them? Confessing that religion was the one thing needful, and recommending it to others with an earnestness, as if they hoped thereby to atone for their own former neglect? We, that are ministers, frequently are witnesses to such things as these.

Whitefield's Sermons (Grand Rapids, MI: Christian Classics Ethereal Library). Sermon: "The Care of the Soul Urged as the One Thing Needful."

———•◦•———

But he is unworthy the name of a minister of the gospel of peace, who is unwilling, not only to have his name cast out as evil, but also to die for the truths of the Lord Jesus.

I know we had more comfort in Moorfields, on Kennington Commons, especially when the rotten eggs, the cats and dogs were thrown upon me, and my gown was filled with clods of dirt that I could scarce move it. I have had more comfort in this burning bush, than when I had been at ease. I remember when I was preaching at Exeter, a stone came and made my forehead bleed, I found at that very time the word came with double power to a laborer that was gazing at me, who was wounded at the same time by another stone. I felt for the lad more than for myself, went to a friend, and the lad came to me. "Sir," says he, "the man gave me a wound but Jesus healed me; I never had my bonds broke till I had my head broke."

I appeal to you whether you were not better when it was colder than now, because your nerves were braced up; you have a day like a dog-day, now you are weak, and are obliged to fan yourselves: thus it is prosperity lulls the soul, and I fear Christians are spoiled by it.

20 Centuries of Great Preaching; Volume 3 (Waco, TX: Word Books Publishing, 1974), p. 114.

There I was honored with having stones, dirt, rotten eggs, and pieces of dead cats thrown at me.

Sodom Had No Bible, by Leonard Ravenhill (Minneapolis, MN: Bethany House Publishers, 1984), p. 187.

———•••———

The open air preacher is at times subjected to great indignities. I have had experiences that I cannot put in print, and wouldn't share in mixed company. — Ray Comfort

Now the furnace is a hot place, and they that are tried in the furnace must be burnt surely. Now what must the Christian burn with? With tribulation and persecution. I heard a person not long ago say, "I have no enemies." Bishop Latimer came to a house one day, and the man of the house said, he had not met with a cross in all his life; give me my horse, says the good bishop, I am sure God is not here where no cross is.

20 Centuries of Great Preaching; Volume 3 (Waco, TX: Word Books Publishing, 1974), pp. 131-132.

———•••———

When you're preaching open air, don't let angry reactions from the crowd concern you. A dentist knows where to work on a patient when he touches a raw nerve. When you touch a raw nerve in the heart of the sinner, it means that you are in business. Anger is a thousand times better than apathy. Anger is a sign of conviction. If I have an argument with my wife and suddenly realize that I am in the wrong, I can come to her in a repentant attitude and apologize, or I can save face by lashing out in anger.

Read Acts 19 and see how Paul was a dentist with an eye for decay. He probed raw nerves wherever he went. At one point, he had to be carried shoulder height by soldiers because of the "violence of the people" (Acts 21:36). Now

that is a successful preacher! He didn't seek the praise of men. John Wesley told his evangelist trainees that when they preached, people should either get angry or get converted. No doubt, he wasn't speaking about the "Jesus loves you" Gospel, but about sin, Law, righteousness, judgment, and Hell.

Whenever you are in an open air situation, be suspicious of so-called Christians who are intent on distracting workers from witnessing. They argue about prophecy, how much water one should baptize with, or in whose name they should be baptized. It is grievous to see five or six Christians standing around arguing with some sectarian nitpicker while sinners are sinking into Hell.

There is one passage in Scripture to which I point for all those who want to witness or preach in the open air. It is 2 Timothy 2:24-26. Memorize it. Scripture tells us that sinners are blind. They cannot see. What would you think if I were to stomp up to a blind man who had just stumbled, and say, "Watch where you're going, blind man!"? Such an attitude is completely unreasonable. The man cannot see. The same applies to the lost—spiritual sight is beyond their ability. Look at the words used in Scripture: "Except a man be born again, he cannot see the kingdom of God ... The god of this world has blinded the minds of them which believe not ... But the natural man receives not the things of the Spirit of God: for they are foolishness to him: neither can he know them ... Having the understanding darkened ... because of the blindness of their heart ... Ever learning, and never able to come to the knowledge of the truth." With these thoughts in mind, read 2 Timothy 2:24-26 again and look at the adjectives used by Paul to describe the attitude we are to have with sinners: "must not strive ... be gentle ... patient ... in meekness." Just as it is unreasonable to be impatient with a blind man, so it is with the sinner.

The Bible warns us to avoid foolish questions because they start arguments (2 Timothy 2:23). Most of us have fallen into the trap of jumping at every objection to the Gospel. However, these questions can often be arguments in disguise to sidetrack you from the "weightier matters of the Law." While apologetics (arguments for God's existence, creation vs. evolution, etc.) are legitimate in evangelism, they should merely be "bait," with the Law of God being the "hook" that brings the conviction of sin. Those who witness solely in the realm of apologetic argument may just get an intellectual decision rather than a repentant conversion. The sinner may come to a point of acknowledging that the Bible is the Word of God, and Jesus is Lord—but even the devil knows that. Always pull the sinner back to his responsibility before God on Judgment Day, as Jesus did in Luke 13:1-5.
— Ray Comfort

Now we have many enemies, but at death they are all lost; they cannot follow us beyond the grave: and this is a great encouragement to us not to regard the scoffs and jeers of the men of this world.

Whitefield's Sermons (Grand Rapids, MI: Christian Classics Ethereal Library). Sermon: "A Penitent Heart, the Best New Year's Gift."

And if after our work is over, our Lord should call us to lay down our lives for the brethren, and to seal the truth of our doctrine with our blood, it would certainly be the highest honor that can be put upon us. "To you it is given not only to believe, but also to suffer," says the apostle to the Philippians.

Whitefield's Sermons (Grand Rapids, MI: Christian Classics Ethereal Library). Sermon: "The Resurrection of Lazarus."

There is an irreconcilable enmity between the seed of the woman, and the seed of the serpent. And if we are not of the world, but show by our fruits that we are of the number of those whom Jesus Christ has chosen out of this world, for that very reason the world will hate us. As this is true of every particular Christian, so it is true of every Christian church in general. For some years past we have heard but little of a public persecution: Why? Because but little of the power of godliness has prevailed amongst all denominations. The strong man armed has had full possession of most professors' hearts, and therefore he has let them rest in a false peace. But we may assure ourselves, when Jesus Christ begins to gather in His elect in any remarkable manner, and opens an effectual door for preaching the everlasting gospel, persecution will flame out, and Satan and his emissaries will do their utmost (though all in vain) to stop the work of God. Thus it was in the first ages, thus it is in our days, and thus it will be, till time shall be no more … Christians and Christian churches must then expect enemies.

Whitefield's Sermons (Grand Rapids, MI: Christian Classics Ethereal Library). Sermon: "Saul's Conversion."

He, who will not contentedly suffer great things for preaching Christ, is not worthy of him. Suffering will be found to be the best preferment, when we are called to give an account of our ministry at the great day.

Whitefield's Sermons (Grand Rapids, MI: Christian Classics Ethereal Library). Sermon: "Saul's Conversion."

Opposition never yet did, or ever will hurt, a sincere convert. Nothing like opposition to make the man of God perfect. None but a hireling, who cares not for the sheep, will be frightened at the approach or barking of wolves. Christ's ministers are as bold as lions: it is not for such men as they to flee.

Whitefield's Sermons (Grand Rapids, MI: Christian Classics Ethereal Library). Sermon: "Saul's Conversion."

We cannot be Christians without being opposed: no; disciples in general must suffer; ministers in particular must suffer great things. But let not thus move any of us from our steadfastness in the gospel.

Whitefield's Sermons (Grand Rapids, MI: Christian Classics Ethereal Library). Sermon: "Saul's Conversion."

And, if I may speak my own experience, I never enjoy more rich communications from God than when despised and rejected of men for the sake of Jesus Christ. However little they may design it, my enemies are my greatest friends. What I most fear, is a calm; but the enmity that is in the hearts of natural men against Christ, will not suffer them to be quiet long. No, as I hope the work of God will increase, so the rags of men and devils will increase also. Let us put on, therefore, the whole armor of God: let us not fear the face of men: "Let us fear him only, who can destroy both body and soul in Hell." I say unto you let us fear Him alone.

Whitefield's Sermons (Grand Rapids, MI: Christian Classics Ethereal Library). Sermon: "Saul's Conversion."

Nothing brings out the enemies of Christ like open air preaching. If you find opposition from within the crowd, don't be distracted from your course. Charles Spurgeon's "Preach Christ or nothing: don't dispute or discuss except with your eye on the cross" is good advice. This doesn't mean that you shouldn't answer questions. It means that you shouldn't be distracted from your objective. When friends and I have been tag-preaching, we would often walk past the preacher and tap him on the ankle to remind him that he was being distracted down an evolutionary rabbit trail. It was something each off us often needed. Evolution and other subjects may tickle the intellect, but they don't address the conscience. God's Law does. — *Ray Comfort*

Value not ... the contempt of friends, which you must necessarily meet with upon your open profession to act according to this determination. For your Master, whose you are, was despised before you; and all that will know nothing else but Jesus Christ, and Him crucified, must, in some degree or other, suffer persecution. It is necessary that offenses should come, to try what is in our hearts, and whether we will be faithful soldiers of Jesus Christ or not.

Whitefield's Sermons (Grand Rapids, MI: Christian Classics Ethereal Library). Sermon: "The Knowledge of Jesus Christ, the Best Knowledge."

———••———

Rejoice ... when you fall into like circumstances; as knowing, that you are therein partakers of the sufferings of Jesus Christ. Consider, that it is necessary such inward trials should come, to wean us from the immoderate love of sensible devotion, and teach us to follow Christ, not merely for His loaves, but out of a principle of love and obedience.

Whitefield's Sermons (Grand Rapids, MI: Christian Classics Ethereal Library). Sermon: "Satan's Devices."

Indeed our modernizers of Christianity would persuade us, that the gospel was calculated only for about two hundred years; and that now there is no need of hating father and mother, or of being persecuted for the sake of Christ and His gospel. But such persons err, not knowing the scriptures, and the power of godliness in their hearts; for whoever receives the love of God in the truth of it, will find, that Christ came to send not peace, but a sword upon earth, as much now as ever. That the father-in-law shall be against the daughter-in-law, in these latter, as well as in the primitive times; and that if we will live godly in Christ Jesus, we must, as then, so now, from carnal friends and relations, suffer persecution.

Whitefield's Sermons (Grand Rapids, MI: Christian Classics Ethereal Library). Sermon: "Satan's Devices."

———••———

The setting about and carrying on the great and necessary work, perhaps may, nay assuredly will expose us also to the ridicule of the unthinking part of mankind, who will wonder, that we run not into the same excess of riot with themselves. And because we deny our sinful appetites, and are not conformed to this world, being commanded in scripture to do the one, and to have our conversation in Heaven, in opposition to the other, they may count our lives folly, and our end to be without honor. But will not the being numbered among the saints, and shining as the stars forever and ever, be a more than sufficient recompense for all the ridicule, lies, or reproach, we can possibly meet with here?

Whitefield's Sermons (Grand Rapids, MI: Christian Classics Ethereal Library). Sermon: "On Regeneration."

———•·•———

They that are born after the flesh will persecute those that are born after the Spirit.

Whitefield's Sermons (Grand Rapids, MI: Christian Classics Ethereal Library). Sermon: "The Heinous Sin of Drunkenness."

———•·•———

Follow him from the manger to the cross, and see whether any persecution was like that which the Son of God, the Lord of Glory, underwent while here on earth. How was He hated by wicked men? How often would that hatred have excited them to lay hold of Him, had it not been for fear of the people? How was He reviled, counted and called a Blasphemer, a Wine-bibber, a Samaritan, nay, a devil, and, in one word, had all manner of evil spoken against Him falsely? What contradiction of sinners did He endure against Himself? How did men separate from His company, and were ashamed to walk with Him openly? Insomuch that He once said to His own disciples, "Will you also go away?" Again, how was He stoned, thrust out of the synagogues, arraigned as a deceiver of the people, a seditious and pestilent fellow, an enemy of

Caesar, and as such scourged, blind-folded, spit upon, and at length condemned, and nailed to an accursed tree?

Thus was the Master persecuted, thus did the Lord suffer; and the servant is not above his Master, nor the disciple above his Lord: "If they have persecuted me, they will also persecute you," says the blessed Jesus. And again, "Every man that is perfect (a true Christian) must be as his Master," or suffer as He did. For in all these things our Lord has set us an example, that we should follow His steps: and therefore, far be it that any, who live godly in Christ Jesus, should henceforth expect to escape suffering persecution.

Whitefield's Sermons (Grand Rapids, MI: Christian Classics Ethereal Library). Sermon: "Persecution, Every Christian's Lot."

Ever since the fall, there has been a irreconcilable enmity between the seed of the woman and the seed of the serpent. Wicked men hate God, and therefore cannot but hate those who are like Him: they hate to be reformed, and therefore must hate and persecute those, who, by a contrary behavior, testify of them, that their deeds are evil.

Whitefield's Sermons (Grand Rapids, MI: Christian Classics Ethereal Library). Sermon: "Persecution, Every Christian's Lot."

You may gather one mark, whereby you may judge whether you are Christians or not. Were you ever persecuted for righteousness sake? If not, you never yet lived godly in Christ our Lord. Whatever you may say to the contrary, the inspired apostle, in the words of the text (the truth of which, I think, I have sufficiently proved) positively asserts, that all who will live godly in Him, shall suffer persecution. Not that all who are persecuted are real Christians; for many sometimes suffer, and are persecuted, on other accounts than for righteousness sake. The great question, therefore, is whether or not you were ever persecuted for living godly?

You may boast of your great prudence and sagacity (and indeed these are excellent things) and glory because you have not run such lengths, and made yourselves so singular, and liable to such contempt, as some others have. But, alas! this is not a mark of your being of a Christian, but of a Laodicean spirit, neither hot nor cold, and sit only to be spewed out of the mouth of God.

That which you call prudence, is often, only cowardice, dreadful hypocrisy, pride of heart, which makes you dread contempt, and afraid to give up your reputation for God. You are ashamed of Christ and His gospel; and in all probability, was He to appear a second time upon earth, in words, as well as works, you would deny Him.

Awake, therefore, all you that live only formally in Christ Jesus, and no longer seek that honor which comes of man. I do not desire to court you, but I entreat you to live godly, and fear not contempt for the sake of Jesus Christ. Beg of God to give you His Holy Spirit, that you may see through, and discover the latent hypocrisy of your hearts, and no longer deceive your own souls. Remember you cannot reconcile two irreconcilable differences, God and Mammon, the friendship of this world with the favor of God.

Know you not who has told you, that 'the friendship of this world is enmity with God?' If therefore you are in friendship with the world, notwithstanding all your specious pretenses to piety, you are at enmity with God: you are only heart-hypocrites; and, "What is the hope of the hypocrite, when God shall take away his soul?" Let the words of the text sound an alarm in your ears; O let them sink deep into your hearts; "Yea, and all that will live godly in Christ Jesus, shall suffer persecution."

Whitefield's Sermons (Grand Rapids, MI: Christian Classics Ethereal Library). Sermon: "Persecution, Every Christian's Lot."

What say you? Are you resolved to live godly in Christ Jesus, notwithstanding the consequence will be, that you must suffer persecution? You are beginning to build; but have you taken our Lord's advice, to "sit down first and count the cost?" Have you well weighed with yourselves that weighty declaration, "He that loves father or mother more than Me, is not worthy of Me;" and again, "Unless a man forsake all that he has he cannot be my disciple?" Perhaps some of you have great possessions; will not you go away sorrowful, if Christ should require you to sell all that you have! Others of you again may be kinsmen, or some way related, or under obligations, to the high priests, or other great personages, who may be persecuting the church of Christ: What say you? Will you, with Moses, "rather choose to suffer affliction with the people of God, than enjoy the pleasures of sin for a season?"

Perhaps you may say, "my friends will not oppose me." That is more than you know: in all probability your chief enemies will be those of your own household. If therefore they should oppose you, are you willing naked to follow a naked Christ? And to wander about in sheep-skins and goats-skins, in dens and caves of the earth; being afflicted, destitute, tormented, rather than not be Christ's disciples? You are now all following with zeal, as Ruth and Orpah did Naomi, and may weep under the word; but are not your tears, crocodile tears?

And, when difficulties come, will you not go back from following your Lord, as Orpah departed from following Naomi? Have you really the root of grace in your hearts? Or, are you only stony-ground hearers? You receive the word with joy; but, when persecution arises because of the Word, will you not be immediately offended?

Be not angry with me for putting these questions to you. I am jealous over you, but it is with a godly jealousy: for, alas! how many have put their hands to the plough, and afterwards have shamefully looked back? I only deal with you, as our Lord did with the person that said, "Lord, I will follow you wherever you will. The foxes have holes, and the birds of the air have nests, but the son of man, (says he) has not where to lay His head." What say you? Are you willing to endure hardness, and thereby approve yourselves good soldiers of Jesus Christ? You now come on foot out of the towns and villages to hear the word, and receive me as a messenger of God: but will you not by and by cry out, Away with him, away with him; it is not fit such a fellow should live upon the earth?

Perhaps some of you, like Hazael, may say, "Are we dogs, that we should do this?" But, alas! I have met with many unhappy souls, who have drawn back unto perdition, and have afterwards accounted me their enemy, for dealing faithfully with them, though once, if it were possible, they would have plucked out their own eyes, and have given them unto me.

Sit down, therefore, I beseech you, and seriously count the cost, and ask yourselves again and again, whether you count all things but dung and dross, and are willing to suffer the loss of all things, so that you may win Christ, and be found in him.

Whitefield's Sermons (Grand Rapids, MI: Christian Classics Ethereal Library). Sermon: "Persecution, Every Christian's Lot."

Do your earthly friends and parents forsake you? Are you cast out of the synagogues? The Lord shall reveal Himself to you, as to the man that was born blind. Jesus Christ shall take you up. If they carry you to prison, and load you with chains, so that the iron enter into your souls, even there shall Christ send an angel from Heaven to strengthen you, and enable you, with Paul and Silas, to "sing praises at midnight." Are you threatened to be thrown into a den of lions, or cast into a burning fiery furnace, because you will not bow down and worship the beast? Fear not; the God, whom you serve, is able to deliver you: or, if He should suffer the flames to devour your bodies, they would only serve, as so many fiery chariots, to carry your souls to God. Thus it was with the martyrs of old; so that once, when he was burning, cried out, "Come, you Papists, if you want a miracle, here, behold one! This bed of flames is to me a bed of down." Thus it was with almost all that suffered in former times: for Jesus, notwithstanding He withdrew His own divinity from Himself, yet has always lifted up the light of His countenance upon the souls of suffering saints. "Fear not therefore those that can kill the body, and after that have no more that they can do; but fear Him only, who is able to destroy both body and soul in Hell." Dare, dare to live godly in Christ Jesus, though you suffer all manner of persecution.

Whitefield's Sermons (Grand Rapids, MI: Christian Classics Ethereal Library). Sermon: "Persecution, Every Christian's Lot."

Do not be discouraged, or think hard of the ways of God, my dear brethren, because you are not loved by the men of this world. If you were of the world, it would love you. It would then be pleased with your company; it would not thrust you from a tavern, or an alehouse; it would not dislike you for singing the songs of the drunkard, or for going to plays, balls, or other polite and fashionable entertainments, as they are called. No, these the children of the world like. But if you will sing hymns and psalms, and go to hear what God has to say unto your souls, and spend your time in reading, praying, and frequenting religious assemblies, then it is that they dislike you, and thrust you out of their company, as unworthy thereof. But let none of these things move you, for the rest which Jesus Christ has prepared for you, is an ample recompense for all you may meet with here.

Whitefield's Sermons (Grand Rapids, MI: Christian Classics Ethereal Library). Sermon: "An Exhortation to the People of God Not to Be Discouraged in Their Way, by the Scoffs and Contempt of Wicked Men."

Warfare

R esolve for Christ, resolve against the devil and his works, and go on fighting the Lord's battles against the devil and his emissaries; attack him in the strongest holds he has, fight him as men, as Christians, and you will soon find him to be a coward; resist him and he will fly from you.

Whitefield's Sermons (Grand Rapids, MI: Christian Classics Ethereal Library). Sermon: "A Penitent Heart, the Best New Year's Gift."

O that the God of love may fill us with such peace and such joy, that every storm, every trial, every temptation we meet with may be overruled to good for us; all our afflictions, all our temptations, are to make Heaven more desirable, and earth more loathsome.

20 Centuries of Great Preaching; Volume 3 (Waco, TX: Word Books Publishing, 1974), p. 126

There is not one single saint in paradise, amongst the goodly fellowship of the prophets, the glorious company of the apostles, the noble army of martyrs, and the spirits of just men made perfect, who, when on earth, was not assaulted by the fiery darts of that wicked one, the devil.

Whitefield's Sermons (Grand Rapids, MI: Christian Classics Ethereal Library). Sermon: "Satan's Devices."

Why, you that are unregenerate must go to Hell, for all your unregenerate relations are there. Your father, the devil, is there, all damned angels and damned spirits are there, your brothers and sisters are there; as they went one way here, so they must be banished from Jesus Christ to one place hereafter.

20 Centuries of Great Preaching; Volume 3 (Waco, TX: Word Books Publishing, 1974), p. 121.

———•◦•———

For as you carry about in you the devil's image, with devils you must dwell: being of the same nature, you must share the same doom.

Whitefield's Sermons (Grand Rapids, MI: Christian Classics Ethereal Library). Sermon: "Marks of Having Received the Holy Ghost."

We may easily judge whose children they are, who love to make a lie, who speak evil of and slander their neighbor, and whose hearts are full of pride, subtlety, malice, envy, revenge, and all uncharitableness. Surely they have Satan for their father: for the tempers of Satan they know, and the works of Satan they do. But were they to see either themselves, or Satan as he is, they could not but be terrified at their own likeness, and abhor themselves in dust and ashes.

Whitefield's Sermons (Grand Rapids, MI: Christian Classics Ethereal Library). Sermon: "Satan's Devices."

———•◦•———

You are children of the devil, if Christ is not in you, if God has not spoken peace to your heart. Poor soul! What a cursed condition are you in. I would not be in your case for ten thousand, thousand worlds. Why? You are just hanging over Hell. What peace can you have when God is your enemy, when the wrath of God is abiding upon your poor soul? Awake, then, you that are sleeping in a false peace, awake, you carnal professors, you hypocrites that go to church, receive the sacrament, read your Bibles, and never felt the power of God upon your hearts. You that are formal professors, you that are baptized heathens, awake, awake, and do not rest on a false bottom. Blame me not for addressing myself to you; indeed, it is out of love to your souls. I see you are lingering in your Sodom, and wanting to stay there; but I come to you as the angel did to lot, to take you by the hand. Come away, my dear brethren—fly, fly, fly for your lives to Jesus Christ, fly to a bleeding God, fly to a throne of grace; and beg of God to break your hearts, beg of God to convince you of your actual sins, beg of God to convince you of your original sin, beg of God to convince you of your self-righteousness—beg of God to give you faith, and to enable you to close with Jesus Christ. O you that are secure, I must be a son of thunder to you, and O that God may awaken you, though it be with thunder; it is out of love, indeed, that I speak to you.

Whitefield's Sermons (Grand Rapids, MI: Christian Classics Ethereal Library). Sermon: "The Method of Grace."

Preaching Peace, When There is No Peace

The prophet gives a thundering message, that they might be terrified and have some convictions and inclinations to repent; but it seems that the false prophets, the false priests, went about stifling people's convictions, and when they were hurt or a little terrified, they were for daubing over the wound, telling them that Jeremiah was but an enthusiastic preacher, that there could be no such thing as war among them, and saying to people, Peace, peace, be still, when the prophet told them there was no peace. The words, then, refer primarily unto outward things, but I verily believe have also a further reference to the soul, and are to be referred to those false teachers, who, when people were under conviction of sin, when people were beginning to look towards heaven, were for stifling their convictions and telling them they were good enough before.[31] And, indeed, people generally love to have it so; our hearts are exceedingly deceitful, and desperately wicked; none but the eternal God knows how treacherous they are. How many of us cry, Peace, peace, to our souls, when there is no peace! How many are there who are now settled upon their lees, that now think they are Christians, that now flatter themselves that they have an interest in Jesus Christ; whereas if we come to examine their experiences, we shall find that their peace is but a peace of the devil's making—it is not a peace of God's giving—it is not a peace that passes human understanding.

(George Whitefield, "The Method of Grace.")

———•◦•———

It is most frustrating to have a professed Christian speak peace to someone who is under conviction of sin. These people usually see the Christian message as a life-improvement. They don't understand the necessity of using God's Law to show sin in its true light. They see God as a benevolent Father-figure, and so they don't tell sinners to flee from His wrath. They are often ignorant of the Law themselves, and don't see that our hearts are deceitfully wicked. Therefore they don't see "fear" as having any part in a sinner coming to the Savior. To them, the gospel is "God has a wonderful plan for your life, and Jesus died on the cross so that you could have a happy, abundant, joy-filled life."

More than once I have had professing Christians censor me while I was open air preaching, for speaking about sin and wrath. They in turn speak about the "God loves you" message, and receive unified applause from the crowd of sinners. ⟶ *Ray Comfort*

❧✦❧

Conviction Must Go Deep

B ut further: you may be convinced of your actual sins, so as to be made to tremble, and yet you may be strangers to Jesus Christ, you may have no true work of grace upon your hearts. Before ever, therefore, you can speak peace to your hearts, conviction must go deeper; you must not only be convinced of your actual transgressions against the Law of God, but likewise of the foundation of all your transgressions.

(George Whitefield, "The Method of Grace.")

❧✦❧

A Son of Thunder

I know by sad experience what it is to be lulled asleep with a false peace; long was I lulled asleep, long did I think myself a Christian, when I knew nothing of the Lord Jesus Christ. I went perhaps farther than many of you do; I used to fast twice a week, I used to pray sometimes nine times a day, I used to receive the sacrament constantly every Lord's day; and yet I knew nothing of Jesus Christ in my heart, I knew not that I must be a new creature—I knew nothing of inward religion in my soul. And perhaps, many of you may be deceived as I, poor creature, was; and, therefore, it is out of love to you indeed, that I speak to you. O if you do not take care, a form of religion will destroy your soul. You will rest in it, and will not come to Jesus Christ at all. Whereas, these things are only the means, and not the end of religion; Christ is the end of the Law for righteousness to all that believe. O, then, awake, you that are settled on your lees. Awake you Church professors; awake you that have a name to live, that are rich and think you want nothing, not considering that you are poor, and blind, and naked. I counsel you to come and buy of Jesus Christ gold, white raiment, and eye-salve. But, I hope there are some that are a little wounded. I hope God does not intend to let me preach in vain. I hope God will reach some of your precious souls, and awaken some of you out of your carnal security. I hope there are some who are willing to come to Christ, and beginning to think that they have been building upon a false foundation.

(George Whitefield, "The Method of Grace.")

False Brethren

There are more unbelievers within the pale than without the pale of the church; let me repeat it again, you may think of it when I am tossing upon the mighty waters, there are more unbelievers within the pale of the church than without. All are not possessors that are professors; all have not got the thing promised; all are not partakers of the promise, that talk and bless God they have got the promise Savior. I may have him in my mouth and upon my tongue, without having the thing promised, or the blessed promise in my heart.

20 Centuries of Great Preaching; Volume 3 (Waco, TX: Word Books Publishing, 1974), p. 120.

You say you have faith; but how do you prove it? Did you ever hear the Lord Jesus call you by name? Were you ever made to obey the call? Did you ever, like Zaccheus, receive Jesus Christ joyfully into your hearts? Are you influenced by the faith you say you have, to stand up and confess the Lord Jesus before men? Were you ever made willing to own, and humble yourselves for your past offenses? Does your faith work by love, so that you conscientiously lay up, according as God has prospered you, for the support of the poor? Do you give alms of all things that you possess? And have you made due restitution to those you have wronged? If so, happy are you; salvation is come to your souls, you are sons, you are daughters of, you shall shortly be everlastingly blessed with, faithful Abraham. But, if you are not thus minded, do not deceive your own souls. Though you may talk of justification by faith, like angels, it will do you no good; it will only increase your damnation. You hold the truth, but it is in unrighteousness: your faith being without works is dead: you have the devil, not Abraham, for your father. Unless you get a faith of the heart, a faith working by love, with devils and damned spirits shall you dwell for evermore.

Whitefield's Sermons (Grand Rapids, MI: Christian Classics Ethereal Library). Sermon: "The Conversion of Zaccheus."

————•◦•————

As God can send a nation of people no greater blessing than to give them faithful, sincere, and upright ministers, so the greatest curse that God can possibly send upon a people in this world, is to give them over to blind, unregenerate, carnal, lukewarm, and unskilled guides. And yet, in all ages, we find that there have been many wolves in sheep's clothing, many that daubed with untempered mortar, that prophesied smoother things than God did allow. As it was formerly, so it is now; there are many that corrupt the Word of God and deal deceitfully with it. *Whitefield's Sermons*

(Grand Rapids, MI: Christian Classics Ethereal Library). Sermon: "The Method of Grace."

True Believers

This then is to be a Christian indeed; to be in the world, and yet not of it; to have our hands, according to our respective stations in life, employed on earth, and our hearts at the same time fixed on things above. Then, indeed, are we "temples of the living God," when with a humble boldness, we can say with a great and good soldier of Jesus Christ, we are the same in the parlor, as we are in the closet; and can at night throw off our cares, as we throw off our clothes; and being at peace with the world, ourselves, and God, are indifferent whether we sleep or die.

Whitefield's Sermons (Grand Rapids, MI: Christian Classics Ethereal Library). Sermon: "Christians, Temples of the Living God."

———•◦•———

He [Christ] is their Alpha and Omega, their first and last, their beginning and end. They are led by His Spirit, as a child is led by the hand of its father; and are willing to follow the Lamb wherever He leads them. They hear, know, and obey His voice. Their affections are set on things above; their hopes are full of immortality; their citizenship is in Heaven. Being born again of God, they habitually live to, and daily walk with, God. They are pure in heart; and, from a principle of faith in Christ, are holy in all manner of conversation and godliness.

Whitefield's Sermons (Grand Rapids, MI: Christian Classics Ethereal Library). Sermon: "Persecution, Every Christian's Lot."

———•◦•———

For he is not a true Christian, who is only one outwardly; nor have we therefore a right, because we daily profess to believe that Christ rose again the third day from the dead. But, he is a true Christian who is one inwardly; and then only can we be styled true believers, when we not only profess to believe, but have felt the power of our blessed Lord's rising from the dead, by being quickened and raised by His Spirit, when dead in trespasses and sins, to a thorough newness both of heart and life.

Whitefield's Sermons (Grand Rapids, MI: Christian Classics Ethereal Library). Sermon: "The Power of Christ's Resurrection."

The Lamb that died, and was buried, is now risen and exalted, and sits on the right-hand of God the Father. And when He shall come to judge all the world, then, my brethren, it will be seen whether we have deserved the usage the world has given us; then it will be known who are the true followers of the Lord Jesus, and who are madmen and fools.

Whitefield's Sermons (Grand Rapids, MI: Christian Classics Ethereal Library). Sermon: "An Exhortation to the People of God Not to Be Discouraged in Their Way, by the Scoffs and Contempt of Wicked Men."

The New Birth

For by being born again from above, I mean receiving a principle of new life, imparted to our hearts by the Holy Ghost, changing you, giving you new thoughts, new words, new actions, new views, so that old things pass away, and all things become new in our souls.

20 Centuries of Great Preaching; Volume 3 (Waco, TX: Word Books Publishing, 1974), p. 122.

When you read, how the prodigal, in the gospel, was reduced to so low a condition, as to eat husks with swine, and how Nebachadnezzar was turned out, to graze with oxen; I am confident, you pity their unhappy state. And when you hear, how Jesus Christ will say, at the last day, to all that are not born again of God, "Depart from me, you cursed, into everlasting fire, prepared for the devil and his angels," do not your hearts shrink within you, with a secret horror? And if creatures, with only our degree of goodness, cannot bear even the thoughts of dwelling with beasts or devils, to whose nature we are so nearly allied, how do we imagine God, who is infinite goodness, and purity itself, can dwell with us, while we are partakers of both their natures? We might as well think to reconcile Heaven and Hell.

Whitefield's Sermons (Grand Rapids, MI: Christian Classics Ethereal Library). Sermon: "The Indwelling of the Spirit, the Common Privilege of All Believers."

It is true, men for the most part, are orthodox in the common articles of their creed. They believe "there is but one God, and one Mediator between God and men, even the man Christ Jesus;" and that there is no other name given under Heaven, whereby they can be saved, besides His. But then tell them, they must be regenerated, they must be born again, they must be renewed in the very spirit, in the inmost faculties of their minds, ere they can truly call Christ, "Lord, Lord," or have an evidence that they have any share in the merits of His precious blood; and they are ready to cry out with Nicodemus, "How can these things be?" Or with the Athenians, on another occasion, "What will this bumbler say? He seems to be a setter-forth of strange doctrines;" because we preach unto them Christ, and the new-birth.

Whitefield's Sermons (Grand Rapids, MI: Christian Classics Ethereal Library). Sermon: "On Regeneration."

We must be so altered as to the qualities and tempers of our minds, that we must entirely forget what manner of persons we once were. As it may be said of a piece of gold, that was once in the ore, after it has been cleansed, purified and polished, that it is a new piece of gold; as it may be said of a bright glass that has been covered over with filth, when it is wiped, and so become transparent and clear, that it is a new glass. Or, as it might be said of Naaman, when he recovered from his leprosy, and his flesh returned unto him like the flesh of a young child, that he was a new man; so our souls, though still the same as to offense, yet are so purged, purified and cleansed from their natural dross, filth and leprosy, by the blessed influences of the Holy Spirit, that they may be properly said to be made anew.

Whitefield's Sermons (Grand Rapids, MI: Christian Classics Ethereal Library). Sermon: "On Regeneration."

Since there is such an infinite disparity, can anyone conceive how a filthy, corrupted, polluted wretch can dwell with an infinitely pure and holy God, before he is changed, and rendered, in some measure, like Him? Can He, who is of purer eyes than to behold iniquity, dwell with it? Can He, in whose sight the heavens are not clean, delight to dwell with uncleanness itself? No, we might as well suppose light to have communion with darkness, or Christ to have concord with Belial.

Whitefield's Sermons (Grand Rapids, MI: Christian Classics Ethereal Library). Sermon: "On Regeneration."

It is very observable, that our divine Master, in the famous passage before referred to, concerning the absolute necessity of regeneration, does not say, Unless a man be born again, he *shall not*, but "unless a man be born again, he *cannot* enter into the kingdom of God." It is founded in the very nature of things, that unless we have dispositions wrought in us suitable to the objects that are to entertain us, we can take no manner of complacency or satisfaction in them. For instance, what delight can the most harmonious music afford to the deaf, or what pleasure can the most excellent picture give to a blind man? Can a tasteless palate relish the richest dainties, or a filthy swine is pleased with the finest garden of flowers? No: and what reason can be assigned for it? An answer is ready;

because they have neither of them any tempers of mind correspondent or agreeable to what they are to be diverted with. And thus it is with the soul hereafter; for death makes no more alteration in the soul, than as it enlarges its faculties, and makes it capable of receiving deeper impressions either of pleasure or pain. If it delighted to converse with God here, it will be transported with the sight of His glorious Majesty hereafter. If it was pleased with the communion of saints on earth, it will be infinitely more so with the communion and society of holy angels, and the spirits of just men made perfect in Heaven. But if the opposite of all this be true, we may assure ourselves the soul could not be happy, was God Himself to admit it (which He never will do) into the regions of the blessed.

Whitefield's Sermons (Grand Rapids, MI: Christian Classics Ethereal Library). Sermon: "On Regeneration."

If we reflect indeed on the first and chief end of our blessed Lord's coming, we shall find it was to be a propitiation for our sins, to give his life a ransom for many. But then, if the benefits of our dear Redeemer's death were to extend no farther than barely to procure forgiveness of our sins, we should have as little reason to rejoice in it, as a poor condemned criminal that is ready to perish by some fatal disease, would have in receiving a pardon from his judge. For Christians would do well to consider, that there is not only a legal hindrance to our happiness, as we are breakers of God's Law, but also a moral impurity in our natures, which renders us incapable of enjoying Heaven … till some mighty change has been wrought in us. It is necessary therefore, in order to make Christ's redemption complete, that we should have a grant of God's Holy Spirit to change our natures, and so prepare us for the enjoyment of that happiness our Savior has purchased by His precious blood.

Whitefield's Sermons (Grand Rapids, MI: Christian Classics Ethereal Library). Sermon: "On Regeneration."

Nothing has done more harm to the Christian world, nothing has rendered the cross of Christ of less effect, than a vain supposition, that religion is something without us. Whereas we should consider, that everything that Christ did outwardly, must be done over again in our souls; or otherwise, the believing there was such a divine person once on earth, who triumphed over Hell and the grave, will profit us no more, than believing there was once such a person as Alexander, who conquered the world.

As Christ was born of the Virgin's womb, so must He be spiritually formed in our hearts. As He died for sin, so must we die to sin. And as He rose again from the dead, so must we also rise to a divine life.

Whitefield's Sermons (Grand Rapids, MI: Christian Classics Ethereal Library). Sermon: The Power of Christ's Resurrection."

For we are but dead men, we are like so many carcasses wrapped up in grave clothes, till that same Jesus who called Lazarus from his tomb, and at whose own resurrection many that slept arose, does raise us also by his quickening Spirit from our natural death, in which we have so long lain, to a holy and heavenly life.

Whitefield's Sermons (Grand Rapids, MI: Christian Classics Ethereal Library). Sermon: "The Power of Christ's Resurrection."

I take it for granted you believe religion to be an inward thing; you believe it to be a work in the heart, a work wrought in the soul by the power of the Spirit of God. If you do not believe this, you do not believe your Bibles. If you do not believe this, though you have got your Bibles in your hand, you hate the Lord Jesus Christ in your heart; for religion is everywhere represented in Scripture as the work of God in the heart.

Whitefield's Sermons (Grand Rapids, MI: Christian Classics Ethereal Library. Sermon: "The Method of Grace.")

Compassion

Tonight somebody sits up with the prisoners; if they find any of them asleep or no sign of them being awake, they knock and call, and the keepers cry, awake! And I have heard that the present ordinary sits up with them all the night before their execution. Therefore, don't be angry with me if I knock at your doors, and cry, poor sinners, awake! Awake! And God help you to take care you do not sleep in an unconverted state tonight. The court is just sitting, the executioner stands ready, and before tomorrow, long before tomorrow, Jesus may say of some of you, "bind him hand and foot." The prisoners tomorrow will have their hands tied behind them, their thumb strings must be put on, and their fetters knocked off. They must be tied fast to the cart, the cap put over their faces, and the dreadful signal given: if you were their relations, would not you weep? Don't be angry then with a poor minister for weeping over them that will not weep for themselves.

20 Centuries of Great Preaching; Volume 3 (Waco, TX: Word Books Publishing, 1974), p. 145.

Drunkenness

Thousands, and I could almost say ten thousands, fall daily at our right-hand, by this sin of drunkenness, in our streets. Nay, men seem to have made a covenant with Hell, and though the power of the civil magistrate is exerted against them, nay, though they cannot but daily see the companions of their riot hourly, by this sin, brought to the grave, yet "they will rise up early to follow strong drink, and cry, Tomorrow shall be as today, and so much the more abundantly; when we awake, we will seek it yet again." It is high time therefore, for your ministers, O God, to lift up their voices like a trumpet; and since human threats cannot prevail, to set before them the terrors of the Lord, and try if these will not persuade them to cease from the evil of their doings.

Whitefield's Sermons (Grand Rapids, MI: Christian Classics Ethereal Library). Sermon: "The Heinous Sin of Drunkenness."

When the apostle would dissuade the Corinthians from fornication, he urges this as an argument, "Flee fornication, brethren; for he that commits fornication, sins against his own body." And may not I as justly cry out, "Flee drunkenness, my brethren, since he that commits that crime, sins against his own body?" For, from where comes so many diseases and distempers in your bodies? Come they not from hence, even from your intemperance in drinking? Who has pains in the head? Who has rottenness in the bones? Who has redness of eyes? He that tarries long at the wine, he that rises early to seek new wine. How many walking skeletons have you seen, whose bodies were once exceeding fair to look upon, fat and well-favored; but, by this sin of drinking, how has their beauty departed from them, and how have they been permitted to walk to and fro upon the earth, as though God intended to set them up, as he did Lot's wife, for monuments of his justice, that others might learn not to get drunk? Nay, I appeal to yourselves: are not many, for this cause, even now sickly among you? And have not many of your companions, whom you once saw so flourishing, like green bay trees, been brought by it with sorrow to their graves?

We might, perhaps, think ourselves hardly dealt with by God, was He to send us, as He did the royal Psalmist, to choose one plague out of three, whereby we should be destroyed. But had the Almighty decreed to cut off man from the face of the earth and to shorten his days, he could not well send a more effectual plague, than to permit men, as they pleased, to overcharge themselves with drunkenness; for though it be a slot, yet it is a certain poison. And if the sword has slain its thousands, drunkenness has slain its ten thousands.

Whitefield's Sermons (Grand Rapids, MI: Christian Classics Ethereal Library). Sermon: "The Heinous Sin of Drunkenness."

But do not despair; for what is impossible with man, is possible with God. Of whom then should you seek for succor, but of Him your Lord? Who, though for this sin of drunkenness, He might justly turn away His face from you ... If you pour out your hearts before Him in *daily prayer*, and ask assistance from above, it may be God will endue you with power from on high, and make you more than conquerors through Jesus Christ. Had you kept up communion with Him in prayer, you would not so long, by drunkenness, have had communion with devils. But, like the Prodigal, you have desired to be your own masters; you have lived without prayer, depended on your own strength; and now see, alas! on what a broken reed you have leaned. How soon have you made yourselves like the beasts that have no understanding? But turn you, turn you from your evil ways. Come to him with the repenting Prodigal saying, "Father we have sinned; we beseech you, let not this sin of drunkenness have any longer dominion over us." Lay hold on Christ by faith, and lo! It shall happen to you even as you will.

Whitefield's Sermons (Grand Rapids, MI: Christian Classics Ethereal Library. Sermon: "The Heinous Sin of Drunkenness.")

Wholly Dedicated

For did He come down from Heaven, and shed His precious blood, to purchase these hearts of ours, and shall we only give Him half of them? O how can we say we love Him, when our hearts are not wholly with Him? How can we call Him our Savior, when we will not endeavor sincerely to approve ourselves to Him, and so let Him see the travail of His soul, and be satisfied! Had any of us purchased a slave at a most expensive rate, and who was before involved in the utmost miseries and torments, and so must have continued forever, had we shut up our bowels of compassion from him; and was this slave afterwards to grow rebellious, or deny giving us but half his service; how, how should we exclaim against his base ingratitude! And yet this base ungrateful slave you are. O man, who acknowledges yourself to be redeemed from infinite unavoidable misery and punishment by the death of Jesus Christ, and yet will not give yourself wholly to Him. But shall we deal with God our Maker in a manner we would not be dealt with by a man like ourselves?

Whitefield's Sermons (Grand Rapids, MI: Christian Classics Ethereal Library. Sermon: "The Almost Christian.")

O let us scorn all base and treacherous treatment of our King and Savior, of our God and Creator. Let us not take some pains all our lives to go to Heaven, and yet plunge ourselves into Hell as last. Let us give to God our whole hearts, and no longer halt between two opinions. If the world be God, let us serve that; if pleasure be a God, let us serve that; but if the Lord He be God, let us, O let us serve Him alone. *Whitefield's Sermons* (Grand Rapids, MI: Christian Classics Ethereal Library. Sermon: "The Almost Christian.")

Christian Service

Nothing is more generally known than our duties which belong to Christianity; and yet, how amazing is it, nothing is less practiced? An idle person tempts the devil to tempt him.

(*20 Centuries of Great Preaching; Volume 3*, Waco, TX: Word Books Publishing, 1974, p. 166.)

———•◦•———

And can you do too much for the Lord Jesus Christ, who has done so much for you? His love to you is unfathomable. O the height, the depth, the length and breadth of this love, that brought the King of Glory from His throne, to die for such rebels as we are, when we had acted so unkindly against Him, and deserved nothing but eternal damnation. He came down and took our nature upon Him. He was made of flesh and dwelt among us; He was put to death on our account; He paid our ransom: surely this should make us rejoice in Him, and not do as too many do, and as we ourselves have too often, crucify this Jesus afresh. Let us do all we can, my dear brethren, to honor Him.

Whitefield's Sermons (Grand Rapids, MI: Christian Classics Ethereal Library). Sermon: "A Penitent Heart, the Best New Year's Gift."

———•◦•———

How may all Christ's ministers strengthen themselves with this consideration, that so long as God hath work for them to do, they are immortal!

Whitefield's Sermons (Grand Rapids, MI: Christian Classics Ethereal Library). Sermon: "The Resurrection of Lazarus."

———•◦•———

If Christ be the Alpha and Omega of all our actions, then our least are acceptable sacrifices. But if this principle be wanting, our most pompous services avail nothing. We are but spiritual idolater; we sacrifice to our own net; we make an idol of ourselves, by making ourselves, and not Christ, the end of our actions. And, therefore, such actions are so far from being accepted by God.

Whitefield's Sermons (Grand Rapids, MI: Christian Classics Ethereal Library). Sermon: "The Knowledge of Jesus Christ, the Best Knowledge."

For, if we have not charity, we are not Christians: charity is the great duty of Christians ... if you have no compassion, you are not true disciples of the Lord Jesus Christ.

(*Whitefield's Sermons*, Grand Rapids, MI: Christian Classics Ethereal Library. Sermon: "The Great Duty of Charity Recommended.")

The World Verses Christ and the Church

T he spirit of the world is hatred; that of Christ is love; the spirit of the world is vexation; that of Christ is pleasure: the spirit of the world is sorrow; that of Christ is joy: the spirit of the world is evil, and that of Christ is good: the spirit of the world will never satisfy us, but Christ's spirit is all satisfaction: the spirit of the world is misery; that of Christ is ease. In one word, the spirit of the world has nothing lasting; but the spirit of Christ is durable, and will last though an eternity of ages. The spirit of Christ will remove every difficulty, satisfy every doubt, and be a means of bringing you to Himself, to live with Him forever and ever.

Whitefield's Sermons (Grand Rapids, MI: Christian Classics Ethereal Library). Sermon: "Christ, the Only Preservative Against a Reprobate Spirit."

While they are singing the songs of the drunkard, you are singing psalms and hymns. While they are at a playhouse, you are hearing a sermon: while they are drinking, reveling and misspending their precious time, and hastening on their own destruction, you are reading, praying, meditating, and working out your salvation with fear and trembling. This is matter enough for a world to reproach you; you are not polite and fashionable enough for them. If you will live godly, you must suffer persecution; you must not expect to go through this world without being persecuted and reviled. If you were of the world, the world would love you; for it always loves its own; but if you are not of the world, it will hate you. It has done so in all ages. It never loved any but those who were pleased with its vanities and allurements. It has been the death of many a lover of Jesus, merely because they have loved Him: And, therefore, my brethren, do not be surprised if you meet with a fiery trial, for all those things will be a means of sending you to your Master the sooner.

Whitefield's Sermons (Grand Rapids, MI: Christian Classics Ethereal Library). Sermon: "Christ, the Only Preservative Against a Reprobate Spirit."

The Church

T he bush was burning, why might it not be a tall cedar, why might it not be some large or some glorious tree, why should the great God choose a bush, a little bush of briars and thorns, above any other thing? But because the church of Christ generally consists of poor, mean, despicable creatures: though it is all glorious within, yet it is all despicable without. It is observed, that when the church came to prosper when Constantine smiled on it, it was soon hugged to death; and that great poet, Milton, observes, that when that emperor gave ministers rich vestments, high honors, great livings, and golden pulpits, there was a voice heard from Heaven, saying, this day there is poison come into the church.

20 Centuries of Great Preaching; Volume 3 (Waco, TX: Word Books Publishing, 1974), p. 130.

Prayer

O prayer! Prayer! It brings and keeps God and man together. It raises man up to God, and brings God down to man. If you would therefore, O believers, keep up your walk with God; pray, pray without ceasing. Be much in secret prayer, set prayer. And when you are about the common business of life, be much in ejaculatory prayer, and send, from time to time, short letters post to Heaven upon the wings of faith. They will reach the very heart of God, and return to you again loaded with spiritual blessings.

20 Centuries of Great Preaching; Volume 3 (Waco, TX: Word Books Publishing, 1974), p. 152.

The way to have the soul transformed, changed into, and made like unto God, is frequently to converse with God. We say a man is as his company. Persons by conversing together, frequently catch each others tempers: and if you have a mind to imbibe the divine temper, pray much.

Whitefield's Sermons (Grand Rapids, MI: Christian Classics Ethereal Library). Sermon: "Christ's Transfiguration."

And I observe this for the comfort of some weak, but real Christians, who think they never pray, unless they can have a great flow of words. But this is a great mistake: for we often pray best, when we can speak least. There are times when the heart is too big to speak: and the spirit itself makes intercession for the saints, and that to according to the will of God, with groanings that cannot be uttered. Such was Hannah's prayer for a son, "She spoke not, only her lips moved:" and such was our Lord's way of praying at this time. And perhaps the soul is never in a better frame, than when in a holy stillness, and unspeakable serenity, it can put itself as a blank in Jesus' hand, for Him to stamp on it just what He pleases.

Whitefield's Sermons (Grand Rapids, MI: Christian Classics Ethereal Library). Sermon: "The Resurrection of Lazarus."

———•◦•———

None of God's children, as one observes, comes into the world stillborn; prayer is the very breath of the new creature: and therefore, if we are prayer-less, we are Christ-less. If we never had the spirit of supplication, it is a sad sign that we never had the spirit of grace in our souls: and you may be assured you never did pray, unless you have felt yourselves sinners, and seen the want of Jesus to be your Savior. May the Lord, whom I serve in the gospel of His dear Son, prick you all to the heart, and may it be said of you all ... behold, they pray!

Whitefield's Sermons (Grand Rapids, MI: Christian Classics Ethereal Library). Sermon: "Saul's Conversion."

———•◦•———

The true believer can no more live without prayer, than without food day by day. And he finds his soul as really and perceptibly fed by the one, as his body is nourished and supported by the other.

Whitefield's Sermons (Grand Rapids, MI: Christian Classics Ethereal Library). Sermon: "Marks of Having Received the Holy Ghost."

———•◦•———

If we would therefore behave like good soldiers of Jesus Christ, we must be always upon our guard, and never pretend to lay down our spiritual weapons of prayer and watching, till our warfare is accomplished by death. For if we do, our spiritual Amalek will quickly prevail against us.

Whitefield's Sermons (Grand Rapids, MI: Christian Classics Ethereal Library). Sermon: "Satan's Devices."

———•◦•———

If we inquire, why there is so little love to be found among Christians, why the very characteristic, by which everyone should know that we are disciples of the holy Jesus, is almost banished out of the Christian world, we shall find it, in great measure, owing to a neglect or superficial performance of that excellent part of prayer, *Intercession,* or imploring the divine grace and mercy in behalf of others.

Whitefield's Sermons (Grand Rapids, MI: Christian Classics Ethereal Library). Sermon: "Intercession, Every Christian's Duty."

You might as reasonably expect to find a living man without breath, as a true Christian without the spirit of prayer and supplication.

Whitefield's Sermons (Grand Rapids, MI: Christian Classics Ethereal Library). Sermon: "Intercession, Every Christian's Duty."

It is the duty of all to pray for their neighbors as much as for themselves, and by all possible acts and expressions of love and affection towards them, at all times, to show their readiness even to lay down their lives for them, if ever it should please God to call them to it.

Whitefield's Sermons (Grand Rapids, MI: Christian Classics Ethereal Library). Sermon: "Intercession, Every Christian's Duty."

The Audience of One

The tide of popularity began to run very high. In a short time I could no longer walk on foot, but was constrained to go in a coach from place to place, to avoid the hosannas of the multitude. They grew quite extravagant in their applauses, and had it not been for my compassionate High Priest, popularity would have destroyed me. I used to plead with Him to take me by the hand and lead me unhurt through this fiery furnace. He heard my request and gave me to see the vanity of all the commendations but His own.

George Whitefield; God's Anointed Servant in the Great Revival of the Eighteenth Century, by Arnold A. Dallimore (Wheaton, IL: Crossway Books, 1990), p. 29.

Servanthood

L et the name of Whitefield perish, but Christ be glorified. Let my name die everywhere, let even my friends forget me, if by that means the cause of the blessed Jesus may be promoted.

George Whitefield; God's Anointed Servant in the Great Revival of the Eighteenth Century, by Arnold A. Dallimore (Wheaton, IL: Crossway Books, 1990), p. 154.

I want to be but the servant of all!

George Whitefield; God's Anointed Servant in the Great Revival of the Eighteenth Century, by Arnold A. Dallimore (Wheaton, IL: Crossway Books, 1990), p. 172.

Men

S ome that are called great men swell till they burst; like study oaks, they think they can stand every wind, till some dreadful storm comes and blows them up by the roots, while the humble reed bends and rises again.

20 Centuries of Great Preaching; Volume 3 (Waco, TX: Word Books Publishing, 1974), p. 129.

You will find that the best of men are men at best.

George Whitefield; God's Anointed Servant in the Great Revival of the Eighteenth Century, by Arnold A. Dallimore (Wheaton, IL: Crossway Books, 1990), p. 147.

Wisdom of This World

H ence it is, that so many, who profess themselves wise, because they can dispute of the causes and effects, the moral fitness and unfitness of things, appear mere fools in the things of God. So that when you come to converse with them about the great work of redemption wrought out for us by Jesus Christ, and of His being a propitiation for our sins, a fulfiller of the covenant of works, and a principle of new life to our souls, they are quite ignorant of the whole matter; and prove, to a demonstration, that, with all their learning, they know nothing yet, as they ought to know. But, alas! how must it surprise a man, when the Most High is about to take away his soul, to think that he has passed for a wise man, and a learned disputer in this world, and yet is left destitute of that knowledge which alone can make him appear with boldness before the judgment-seat of Jesus Christ? How must it grieve him, in a future state, to see others, whom he despised as illiterate men, because they experimentally knew Christ, and him crucified, exalted to the right-hand of God; and himself, with all his fine accomplishments, because he knew everything, perhaps, but Christ, thrust down into Hell?

Whitefield's Sermons (Grand Rapids, MI: Christian Classics Ethereal Library). Sermon: "The Knowledge of Jesus Christ, the Best Knowledge."

Money

M any, both young and old, now-a-days, come running to worship our blessed Lord in public, and kneel before Him in private, and inquire at His gospel, what they must do to inherit eternal life. But when they find they must renounce the self-enjoyment of riches, and forsake all in affection to follow Him, they cry, "The Lord pardon us in this thing! We pray to you, have us excused." But is Heaven so small a trifle in men's esteem, as not to be worth a little gilded earth? Is eternal life so mean a purchase, as not to deserve the temporary renunciation of a few transitory riches? Surely it is. But, however inconsistent such a behavior may be, this inordinate love of money is too evidently the common and fatal cause, why so many are no more than almost Christians.

Whitefield's Sermons (Grand Rapids, MI: Christian Classics Ethereal Library). Sermon: "The Almost Christian."

Wherein does true wisdom consist? Were I to ask some of you, perhaps you would say, in indulging the lust of the flesh, and saying to your souls, eat, drink, and be merry: but this is only the wisdom of brutes; they have as good a gust and relish for sensual pleasures, as the greatest epicure on earth. Others would tell me, true wisdom consisted in adding house to house, and field to field, and calling lands after their own names: but this cannot be true wisdom; for riches often take to themselves wings, and fly away, like an eagle towards Heaven. Even wisdom itself assures us, "that a man's life does not consist in the abundance of the things which he possesses." Vanity, vanity, all these things are vanity; for, if riches leave not the owner, the owners must soon leave them; for rich men must also die, and leave their riches for others.' Their riches cannot procure them redemption from the grave, where we are all hastening apace.

Whitefield's Sermons (Grand Rapids, MI: Christian Classics Ethereal Library). Sermon: "Christ, the Believer's Wisdom, Righteousness, Sanctification and Redemption."

———·•·———

We were created to be a help to each other. God has made no one so independent as not to need the assistance of another. The richest and most powerful man upon the face of this earth needs the help and assistance of those who are around him. And though he may be great today, a thousand accidents may make him as low tomorrow; he that is rolling in plenty today may be in as much scarcity tomorrow. If our rich men would be more charitable to their poor friends and neighbors, it would be a means of recommending them to the favor of others, if Providence should frown upon them. But alas, our great men would much rather spend their money in a playhouse, at a ball, an assembly, or a masquerade, than relieve a poor distressed servant of Jesus Christ. They had rather spend their estates on their hawks and hounds, on their whores, and earthly, sensual, devilish pleasures, than comfort, nourish, or relieve one of their distressed fellow creatures.

Whitefield's Sermons (Grand Rapids, MI: Christian Classics Ethereal Library). Sermon: "The Great Duty of Charity Recommended."

Now, you may think nothing but of your pleasures and delights, of living in ease and plenty, and never consider how many thousands of your fellow creatures would rejoice at what you are making waste of, and setting no account by. Let me beseech you, my rich brethren, to consider the poor of the world, and how commendable and praiseworthy it is to relieve those who are distressed. Consider, how pleasing this is to God, how delightful it is to man, and how many prayers you will have put up for your welfare, by those persons whom you relieve. And let this be a consideration to spare a little out of the abundance wherewith God has blessed you, or the relief of His poor. He could have placed you in their low condition, and they in your high state; it is only His good pleasure that has thus made the difference, and shall not this make you remember your distressed fellow creatures?

Whitefield's Sermons (Grand Rapids, MI: Christian Classics Ethereal Library). Sermon: "The Great Duty of Charity Recommended."

Eternity

L earn, O saints! From what has been said, to sit loose to all your worldly comforts; and stand ready prepared to part with everything, when God shall require it at your hand. Take care of your life and the Lord will take care of your death. Whitefield's Testimony

When I was sixteen years of age, I began to fast twice a week for thirty-six hours together, prayed many times a day, received the sacrament every Lord's Day, fasted myself almost to death all the forty days of Lent, during which, I made it a point of duty never to go less than three times a day to public worship, besides seven times a day to my private prayers, yet I knew no more that I was to be born again in God, born a new creature in Christ Jesus, than if I was never born at all.

I had a mind to be upon the stage, but than I had a qualm of conscience; I used to ask people, "Pray can I be a player, and yet go to the sacrament and be a Christian?" "Oh," say they, "such a one, who is a player, goes to the sacrament; though according to the law of the land, no player should receive the sacrament, unless they give proof that they repent; that was Archbishop Tilotson's doctrine." "Well then, if that be the case," said I, "I will be a player," and I thought to act my part for the devil as well as any body; but, blessed be God, He stopped me in my journey. I must bear testimony to my old friend, Mr. Charles Wesley; he put a book into my hands, called *The Life of God in the Soul of Man*, whereby God showed me, that I must be born again or be damned. I know the place; it may be superstitious, perhaps, but whenever I go to Oxford, I cannot help running to that place where Jesus Christ first revealed Himself to me, and gave me the new birth.

20 Centuries of Great Preaching; Volume 3 (Waco, TX: Word Books Publishing, 1974), p. 115.

I know by sad experience what it is to be lulled asleep with a false peace; long was I lulled asleep, long did I think myself a Christian, when I knew nothing of the Lord Jesus Christ. I went perhaps farther than many of you do; I used to fast twice a-week, I used to pray sometimes nine times a day, I used to receive the sacrament constantly every Lord's-day; and yet I knew nothing of Jesus Christ in my heart, I knew not that I must be a new creature—I knew nothing of inward religion in my soul.

Whitefield's Sermons (Grand Rapids, MI: Christian Classics Ethereal Library). Sermon: "The Method of Grace."

A Notable Conversion

Henry Tanner, born at Exeter, was now in the twenty-sixth year of his age, and was working, at Plymouth, as a shipwright. One day, while at work, he heard, from a considerable distance, the voice of Whitefield, who was preaching in the open air; and, concluding that the man was mad, he and a half dozen of his companions filled their pockets with stones, and set off to knock the preacher down. Whitefield's text was Acts 8:19, 20. Tanner listened with astonishment; and, without using his stones, went home, determined to hear him again next evening. The text, on this occasion, was Luke 24:47; and Tanner was in such an agony of soul, that he was forced to cry, "God be merciful to me a sinner!" The next night, while Whitefield was preaching on "Jacob's Ladder," Tanner found peace with God ... Ten years after his conversion, he removed to Exeter, and began to preach with great success.

(Tyerman, Vol. 2, p.104.)

Whitefield's Preaching

Mrs. Jonathan Edwards was also much taken with Whitefield's ministry. She wrote to her brother, the Rev. James Pierrepont of New Haven, stating, "It is wonderful to see what a spell he casts over an audience by proclaiming the simplest truths of the Bible. I have seen upward of a thousand people hang on his words with breathless silence, broken only by an occasional half-suppressed sob. He impresses the ignorant, and not less the educated and refined ... our mechanics shut up their shops, and the day-laborers throw down their tools to go and hear him preach, and few return unaffected ... Many, very many persons in Northampton date the beginning of new thoughts, new desires, new purposes, and a new life, from the day they heard him preach of Christ ..."

(Excerpt from: *George Whitefield—God's Anointed Servant in the Great Revival of the Eighteenth Century*, p. 89.)

An Early Response

He preaches once a week on the steps of a workhouse, with a hall behind, and a courtyard almost full before. He has preached in two other parts of Kingswood, among the colliers; and thousands come—horsemen, coaches, chaises, etc. Thus the Gospel spreads round the country, for divers come from far—some twenty miles. You may be sure we are set up for being stark mad.

(A letter by William Seward, in Tyerman, Vol. 1, pp. 186-87.)

On February 17, 1739, the fire of the First Great Awakening was sparked. George Whitefield said, "I have now taken the field. Some may censure me, but is there not a cause? Pulpits are denied, and the poor coalminers are ready to perish for lack of knowledge."

Whitefield needed help with his ministry, so he called on his beloved friend, John Wesley. Wesley observed Whitefield preaching open air and said, "I can hardly reconcile myself at first to this strange way of preaching in the fields ... having been all my life, till very lately, so tenacious of every point relating to decency and order, that I should have thought the saving of souls almost a sin, if it had not been done in a church."

However, he became convinced that this was not only biblical, but the most effective way to reach the lost. John Wesley preached about fifteen sermons a week for fifty-three years. He preached over 40,000 sermons and traveled on horseback 220,000 miles to preach open air. If you can find a copy of John Wesley's Journal, it is worth reading. He makes the most zealous of us seem lukewarm. — Ray Comfort

Whitefield's Work Ethic

Had I a hundred hands, I could employ them all. The harvest is very great. I am ashamed I can do no more for Him who has done so much for me.

(Tyerman, Vol. 1, p. 273.)

How Whitefield puts into words how each of us should feel about the gift of life and for the love expressed at the cross. His motivation to reach the lost was fueled by an unending gratitude, and gratitude of those who see the cross can't easily be put into words. ➤ *Ray Comfort*

❦

Whitefield Welcomed to Boston

W hitefield was invited to Boston by the Rev. Dr. Colman, was warmly welcomed by almost all the Bostonians, except a famous doctor of divinity, who met him in the streets, and said, "I am sorry to see *you* here;" and to whom Whitefield quietly remarked, "So is the devil."

(Tyerman, Vol. 1, p. 408.)

❦

Whitefield's Friends

Benjamin Franklin

I t was wonderful to see the change soon made in the manners of our inhabitants; from being thoughtless or indifferent about religion; so that one could not walk through the town in an evening without hearing psalms sung in different families of every street.

20 Centuries of Great Preaching; Volume 3 (Waco, TX: Word Books Publishing, 1974), pp. 108-109.

I happen soon after to attend one of his sermons, in the course of which I perceived he intended to finish with a collection, and I silently resolved that he should get nothing from me. I had in my pocket a handful of copper money, three or four silver dollars, and five pistoles in gold. As he proceeded I began to soften, and concluded to give the coppers. Another stroke of his oratory made me ashamed of that, and determined me to give the silver; and he finished so admirably, that I emptied my pocket wholly into the collector's dish, gold and all.

20 Centuries of Great Preaching; Volume 3 (Waco TX: Word Books Publishing, 1974), p. 109.

He had a loud and clear voice, and articulated his words and sentences so perfectly that he might be heard and understood at a great distance, especially as his audience, however numerous, observed the most exact silence. He preached one evening from the middle of Market Street, and on the West Side of Second Street, which crosses it at right angles. Both streets were filled with his hearers to a considerable distance. Being among the hindmost in Market Place, I had the curiosity to learn how far he could be heard, by retiring backwards down the street towards the river, and I found his voice distinct till I came near Front-Street, when some noise in that Street obscured it. Imagining then a semi-circle, of which my distance should be the radius, and that it were filled with auditors, to each of whom I allowed two square feet, I computed that he might well be heard by more then 30,000. This reconciled me to the newspaper accounts of his having preached to 25,000 people in the fields, and to the ancient histories of Generals haranguing whole armies, of which I had sometimes doubted.

20 Centuries of Great Preaching; Volume 3 (Waco, TX: Word Books Publishing, 1974), pp. 111-112.

Arnold A. Dalllimore

He ... urged all ministers not to be satisfied with preaching on Sundays only, but to do so seven days a week; to preach in the open-air and not to be limited to their own parishes, but to go forth wherever lost souls were found and to proclaim the grace of God to them. Such actions, he assured them, would bring the opposition of authorities and the hatred of the world, but it would also witness the blessing of God.

George Whitefield; God's Anointed Servant in the Great Revival of the Eighteenth Century, by Arnold A. Dallimore (Wheaton, IL: Crossway Books, 1990), p. 166.

Leonard Ravenhill

What was the secret of Whitefield's success? I think three things: he preached a pure gospel, he preached a powerful gospel, he preached a passionate gospel.

Sodom Had No Bible, by Leonard Ravenhill; (Minneapolis, MN: Bethany House Publishers, 1984), p. 188.

Cornelius Winter

He seldom, if ever, got through a sermon without tears.

Sodom Had No Bible, by Leonard Ravenhill; (Minneapolis, MN: Bethany House Publishers, 1984), p. 188.

John Newton

It seemed as though he never preached in vain.

Sodom Had No Bible, by Leonard Ravenhill; (Minneapolis, MN: Bethany House Publishers, 1984), p. 189.

John Wesley

Have we read or heard of any person who called so many thousands, so many myriads of sinners to repentance? Above all, have we read or heard of anyone who has been God's blessed instrument to bring so many sinners from darkness to light and from the power of Satan unto God as Whitefield.

Sodom Had No Bible, by Leonard Ravenhill; (Minneapolis, MN: Bethany House Publishers, 1984), p.189.

William Thayer

Whitefield was a poor boy, and lost his father early in life. To earn an honest penny for his widowed mother, he became bootblack in the University of Oxford. To the professors and students, he was an interesting boy. His whole appearance indicated that he did not mean to black boots for a living all his days. His eyes and ears were opened to learn. Whenever he could catch up a book to read or study, his soul seemed on fire. One day a student found him poring over a Latin grammar. The student asked him how he would like to pursue a course of the study in the institution. On receiving the reply that he could wish for nothing better, the student consented to become his teacher. That was the beginning of a marvelous career. Under the discipline of close application, industry, and perseverance, his intellectual faculties developed rapidly. Nothing was too hard for him: difficulties only increased his determination. Present attainments sharpened his appetite for the highest there was. So he worked, studied, conquered. He spurned mediocrity; the best he sought and found.

Gaining Favor with God and Man, by William Thayer; (San Antonio, TX: Mantle Ministries, 19890, p. 217.

C. H. Spurgeon

It was a brave day for England when Whitefield began field preaching.

George Whitefield; God's Anointed Servant in the Great Revival of the Eighteenth Century, by Arnold A. Dallimore (Wheaton, IL: Crossway Books, 1990), p. 40.

Would you like similar words to be said of you? Then take courage and begin your "field preaching." You don't need permission to enter a pulpit. You don't have to build a sanctuary. Simply find some sinners and preach to them.

While you might think that overcoming your fear of doing this is your big hurdle, it might be that finding a crowd is a bigger problem. If you don't have access to talented singers who are able to gather a crowd, there is perhaps another way to draw them in. It is to give away money. Jesus informed us that there are two things in this world that people love: God or money. He told us that if they don't love God, they will instead love money. It will be their source of joy, their security, and it will be a means of getting their attention. (Jesus often used money to get the attention of His hearers.) He told stories about money; He asked people to show Him money, and He even put some into a fish's mouth to make a point).

Hold ten or twelve dollars in your hand (where they can be seen), and say, "I'm going to give away some money in a few minutes, so gather around. I will ask some simple questions. Get the answer correct, and you get the money!"

*Then ask those who are listening what they think is the greatest killer of drivers in the U.S. This stirs their curiosity. Some begin calling out, "Alcohol!" or "Falling asleep at the wheel!" Tell them it's not, and repeat the question a few more times, saying that you will give a dollar to the person who gets the answer. Tell them that they will **never** guess what kills more drivers than anything else in America.*

A few more shouts emit from the crowd. People are now waiting around for the answer. What kills more drivers than anything else in the United States? What could be the death of you and me? You won't believe this, but it is "trees." Millions of them line our highways, waiting for a driver to kill. When one is struck, the tree stays still, sending the driver into eternity.

Then tell the crowd that you have another question for them. Ask what they think is the most common food on which people choke to death in U.S. restaurants. Over the next few minutes, go through the same scenario. People call out "Steak!" "Chicken bones!" Believe it or not, the answer is "hard-boiled egg yoke."

By now you have a crowd that is enjoying what is going on. Ask them what they think is the most dangerous job in America. Someone calls out "police officer." It's not. Someone else might name another dangerous profession like "firefighter." Say, "Good one ... but wrong." Give a suggestion by saying, "Why doesn't someone say 'electrician'?" Someone takes the suggestion and says, "Electrician!" Say, "Sorry, it's not electrician." The most dangerous job in the United States ... is to be the president. Out of forty or so, four have been murdered while on the job.

Then tell the crowd you have another question. "Does anyone in the crowd consider himself to be a "good person?" By now you will have noted who in the crowd has the self-confidence to speak out. Point to one or two and ask, "Sir, do you consider yourself to be a good person?" The Bible tells us that "every man will proclaim his own goodness" (Proverbs 20:6), and he does. He smiles and says, "Yes, I do consider myself to be a good person." Ask him if he has ever told a lie. Has he stolen, lusted, blasphemed, etc.? That's when all heaven breaks loose. There is conviction of sin. Sinners hear the Gospel, and angels rejoice. — Ray Comfort

More Questions for Drawing a Crowd

Who wrote, "Ask not what your country can do for you. Ask what you can do for your country"? (President Kennedy's speechwriter)."

What is the only fish that can blink with both eyes? (A shark)

Who was John Lennon's first girlfriend? (Thelma Pickles)

How long does it take the average person to fall asleep: 2 minutes, 7 minutes, or 4 hours? (7 minutes)

How long is a goldfish's memory span: 3 seconds, 3 minutes, or 3 hours? (3 seconds)

How many muscles does a cat have in each ear: 2, 32, or 426? (32)

If you have other Christians with you, have them form an audience and look as though they are listening to your preaching. This will encourage others to stop and listen. Tell the Christians to never stand with their backs to the preacher. I have seen open-air meetings when a fellow laborer is preaching for the first time, and what are the Christians doing? They are talking among themselves. Why then should anyone stop and listen if those in front of the speaker aren't even attentive? It is so easy to chat with friends when you've heard the Gospel a million times before. I have found myself doing it, but it is so disheartening for the preacher to speak to the backs of a crowd.

Also, instruct Christians not to argue with hecklers. That will ruin an open-air meeting. I have seen an old lady hit a heckler with her umbrella and turn the crowd from listening to the Gospel to watching the fight she has just started. Who can blame them? Remember, the enemy will do everything he can to distract your listeners. Don't let him.

I t is a poor sermon that gives no offense; that neither makes the hearer displeased with himself nor with the preacher.

Bibliography

Belcher, Joseph George *Whitefield: A Biography, With Special Reference to His Labors in America,* NY: American Tract Society, n.d. (1853).

Dallimore, Arnold A., *George Whitefield; God's Anointed Servant in the Great Revival of the Eighteenth* Century, Wheaton, IL: Crossway Books, 1990.

Dargan, Edwin Charles, *A History Of Preaching,* Grand Rapids: Baker Book House, 1974. Three volumes.

The Journal of the Rev Charles Wesley, MA., Volume 2, Grand Rapids, MI; Baker, 1980.

Murray, Iain H. *Revival and Revivalism: The Making and Marring of American Evangelicalism, 1750-1858,* Edinburgh: Banner Of Truth Trust, 2002.

Ravenhill, Leonard, *Sodom Had No Bible,* Minneapolis, MN: Bethany House Publishers, 1984.

Thayer, William, *Gaining Favor with God and Man,* San Antonio, TX: Mantle Ministries, 1989.

20 Centuries of Great Preaching; Volume 3, Waco, TX: Word Books Publishing, 1974.

Tyerman, Rev. L. *The Life of the Rev. George Whitefield,* Ale: The Need Of The Times Publishers, 1995. Two volumes.

Webber, F. R. *A History of Preaching in Britain and America,* Milwaukee: Northwestern Publishing House, 1952. Three volumes.

Whitefield's Sermons, Grand Rapids, MI: Christian Classics Ethereal Library.
http://www.ccel.org/ccel/whitefield/sermons.ii.html

Whittier, John Greenleaf, *"The Preacher," Complete Poetical Works,* Boston: Houghton Mifflin, 1882.

The World's Greatest Preachers, compiled by Ray Comfort and Kirk Cameron, New Kensington, PA: Whitaker House, 2003.

Subject Index

Don't miss these other helpful publications:

Hell's Best Kept Secret (Whitaker House)

The Way of the Master (Tyndale House Publishers)

What Did Jesus Do? (Genesis Publishing Group)

The Way of the Master for Kids (Genesis Publishing Group)

Behind the Scenes: The Way of the Master (Genesis Publishing Group)

Spurgeon Gold (Bridge-Logos Publishers)

The World's Greatest Preachers (Whitaker House)

The School of Biblical Evangelism textbook (Bridge-Logos Publishers)

How to Win Souls and Influence People (Bridge-Logos Publishers)

God Doesn't Believe in Atheists (Bridge-Logos Publishers)

Out of the Comfort Zone (Bridge-Logos Publishers)

A Full House of Growing Pains (Genesis Publishing Group)

What Hollywood Believes (Genesis Publishing Group)

The Way of the Master Minute: A Devotional for Busy Christians (Bridge-Logos Publishers)

How to Live Forever … Without Being Religious (Bridge-Logos Publishers)

The Evidence Bible (Bridge-Logos Publishers)

Listen to The Way of the Master Radio daily.
See www.WayoftheMaster.com

The Way of the Master
P.O. Box 1172
Bellflower, CA 90706

More **Bridge-Logos** Titles
from Ray Comfort

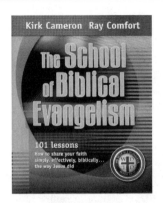

The School of Biblical Evangelism

In this comprehensive study course, you will learn how to share our faith simply, effectively, and biblically … the way Jesus did. Discover the God-given evangelistic tools that will enable you to confidently talk about the Savior.

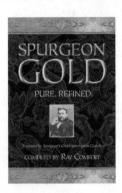

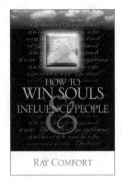

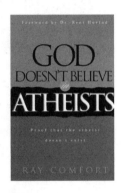

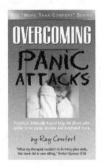

For more information about Ray Comfort,
visit www.livingwaters.com, call 800-437-1893, or write to:
Living Waters Publications, P.O. Box 1172, Bellflower, CA 90706

Pure Gold Classics

BEST-SELLING COLLECTIBLES IN AN EXPANDING SERIES

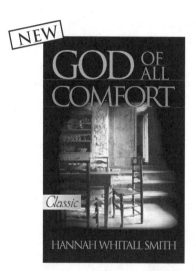

NEW

GOD OF ALL COMFORT

Classic

HANNAH WHITALL SMITH

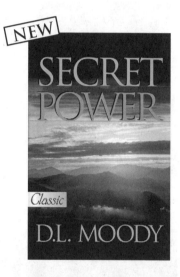

NEW

SECRET POWER

Classic

D.L. MOODY

- Timeline
- Indexes
- Biographies
- Illustrated
- Bible Study
- Collectible
- Modern English

7 Point Advantage

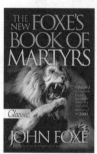

THE NEW FOXE'S BOOK OF MARTYRS

Classic

JOHN FOXE

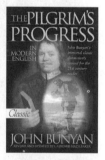

THE PILGRIM'S PROGRESS IN MODERN ENGLISH

Classic

JOHN BUNYAN

THE GREATEST THING IN THE WORLD

Classic

HENRY DRUMMOND

ABSOLUTE SURRENDER

Classic

ANDREW MURRAY

MORNING BY MORNING

Classic

CHARLES H. SPURGEON

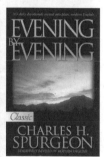

EVENING BY EVENING

Classic

CHARLES H. SPURGEON

SENSITIVELY REVISED IN MODERN ENGLISH

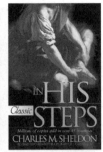
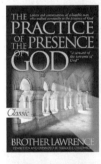
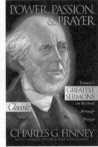
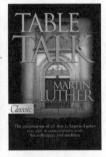
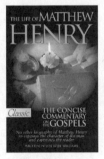
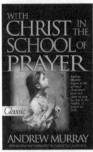
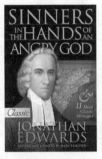

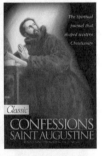
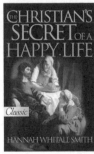
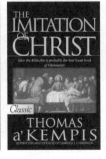
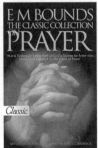
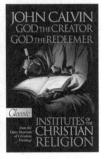

AVAILABLE AT FINE CHRISTIAN BOOKSTORES